The Great British Property Scam

The buy-to-let scandal of the century

Neil Bromage

ISBN-13: 979-8-8068-7439-2

Cover design by: Art Painter

Library of Congress Control Number: 2018675309

Printed in the United States of America

DEDICATION

This book is dedicated to a couple who have worked tirelessly on behalf of hundreds of other investors, who like them have lost significant amounts of money. Ray and Lois Ingham have spent the last few years holding together a substantial, disparate group of people and steering them towards a hopeful recovery of their losses. I know that at times, every minute of the day has seen them bombarded with contacts from people around the world, many of whom had very different desires and understanding of what faced them. Ray and Lois also stuck their necks out for me and UCIS Advice Point in the face of fierce criticism. Their commitment helped us to bring together the current A1 Alpha group of claimants. They have also continued to offer friendship and help when we have spent many hours on the telephone discussing the diverse matters referred to in this book. I will always be grateful to them. Hopefully, one day we may even meet and enjoy a bottle of wine together but whether or not, they will always have my gratitude and thanks.

Introduction

Unlawful property investment schemes have now failed in huge numbers across the UK. Hotel rooms, student accommodation, rooms in care homes, storage pods and car parking spaces have all been sold unlawfully to unwitting investors. At one point even burial plots were being sold in this way. Billions of pounds have been taken from investors, in many cases from their pension or retirement nest egg. Promised high-level returns, many of those investors now face retirement in penury.   It is now widely acknowledged that virtually all these property developments were Unregulated Collective Investment Schemes (UCIS). The Financial Conduct Authority (FCA) is currently investigating and prosecuting the first culprits. Others will follow in their wake as the Serious Fraud Office has also now stepped in.   Schemes like these should have been authorised by the FCA. If they are not a whole range of offences have been committed and are now coming to light. At the same time, many schemes still exist and continue to be marketed by unscrupulous sales teams in the full knowledge that they are UCIS.

6

It was late in 2013 when I was introduced to the idea of buying a hotel and selling off all the bedrooms to investors. A casual acquaintance sat down in our office and told us he was in the process of buying two hotels in Cheshire and how all the bedrooms were being sold to investors for £90,000 - £100,000 each. As catering and hospitality is in my blood my ears quickly pricked up. If he can do it why can`t we, I thought.

We did. We got the t-shirt and an FCA investigation to go with it. "We think you may be running an unregulated collective investment scheme", they said. Thankfully, with the help of very good and very expensive lawyers, we put it right to the satisfaction of the FCA.

Since then, and as in a previous life I was a Legal Executive, my head has been buried in the legislation – The Financial Services and Markets Act 2000 - looking for a compliant way to do what lots of developers are doing illegally. That is until one day, in the late summer of 2019 I realised it doesn`t exist.

Over the last few years, I`ve worked with thousands of investors in the UK and around the world, who have acquired these UCIS products. I was one of the first to openly identify the UCIS element of these schemes. I

7

have a target hit list of more than 450 individual developments which are UCIS and most of which have failed. I was instrumental in pulling together a group of 250-300 investors in the A1 Alpha (£150m +) scheme and enabling them to proceed towards recovering their losses and also a group of around 100+ in the failed Pinnacle scheme. I've dealt with the solicitors, barristers, litigation funders, and insurers who are involved in these significant claims.

I am the poacher turned gamekeeper.

The Great British Property Scam explores the origins of these schemes and how they have slipped under the radar for so long. It will examine failed schemes and look at how they have fallen foul of the legislation. The role of the agents marketing these schemes to the public will be scrutinised, along with that of the all-important lawyers. Real investor stories will bring life to the subject as we look at the effects on their lives. The role of the Insolvency Practitioners is also addressed, reflecting the conflict of interests that are present. Finally, the potential solutions for investors will be made clear with input from law firms and barristers currently working on many cases.

NB. All comments received from investors have been added unedited and without change.

Neil Bromage.

CHAPTER 1

The Poacher Turns Gamekeeper

The best crimes are those you can`t see.

It was late 2013 in the wake of the financial meltdown of 2008. The credit crunch that followed meant that few if any property deals were being funded and our commercial finance brokerage was haemorrhaging cash. At the time of the crash our business pipeline had deals valued at close to one hundred million pounds in progress which would have netted us somewhere close to one and a half million in fees. Seventy-five percent of them were quite easily fundable but not one single deal was completed.

We were broke. We needed another source of income, fast.

I remember the day Mike came to visit us. We met him in the boardroom of the five thousand square foot two-storey office we rattled around and could no longer afford. We had done business successfully with him in the past and considered him an okay sort of guy. He was a property man and after running an estate agency had built up a lucrative portfolio until a fallout with his bank wreaked havoc and he was left playing catch-up. If you`ve been in business, there`s every chance you`ve been there too.

10

Over coffee and catch-up he told us that together with two or three partners he was in the process of buying two hotels in Cheshire, UK, home to footballers, stockbrokers and horsey types. One was on the busy M6 Motorway and the other, just a few miles away on a main trunk road into Manchester, capital of the north. Both were in prime positions with vast amounts of traffic streaming past them on any given day. He explained how all the bedrooms were being sold off to investors in the Far East for £90,000 - £100,000 each. I'd never heard of this concept even though I'm usually up to speed with what's going on in the business world. But as catering and hospitality is in my blood I was really interested. What a great idea! And if he can do it why can't we, I thought.

I haven't a clue why I would think this was a good idea. My family may have owned a couple of hotels in Blackpool, Britain's number one holiday resort and done reasonably well out of them but Blackpool hotels have a longstanding reputation for surviving because they have two sets of accounts. One for the hotelier and one for the taxman. Having never dodged any tax at all that didn't appeal to me. And as most businesses have only ever bought me problems, I really should have stuck to the only thing I've ever done successfully, writing and journalism. But as I said, we were broke.

The worlds of property, finance, and law still carry the baggage of the eighties. Thatcherism and the "Just-do-It" attitude still prevail and the readiness of entrepreneurs to believe a scheme will work is at times astounding. The goals remain the same today as they were back then and very little has changed. Everyone still wants to be seen at the same exclusive club, drive the same gas-guzzling 4x4 with blacked-out windows and holiday in St Lucia. The only difference today is that everyone is a lot smarter, particularly those who lacked any scruples to begin with.

Mike introduced us to the two men who would put these hotel schemes together and I met them at what I believed to be their hotel in Harrogate, North Yorkshire. The town is well known for a variety of exhibitions and conferences and is quite affluent. The Kimberley Hotel was again well positioned, immediately next door to the Harrogate Conference Centre, home to many of those events. The property was substantial and impressive. And so were they.

I guessed by the numberplates that the Range Rover and Mercedes parked back and front of the hotel were probably theirs and they had sharp expensive suits to match. Stewart Lewis bore a resemblance to the late (Lord) Lew Grade. His much shorter sidekick, Steve Gaunt, had a more oily, entrepreneurial look and I could imagine him greased up and broiling on a sun-lounger in Marbella. Twins they most definitely were not. But it's a tag that sticks.

They had apparently done this before, and not only with hotels. Gaunt also owned, allegedly, an even more impressive pile, Dunchurch Park Hotel in Rugby, Warwickshire, where all the rooms had also been sold to investors. At the time of writing both hotels have been closed and the Harrogate property is in administration.

They lunched me and took me through the whole process. They would introduce us to the sales team, London based RW Invest who had also done this on many previous occasions (and continue to do so) and provide all the necessary legal documentation for our solicitors to use. All of which, they claimed, had been drafted by a Magic Circle Law Firm – the top five firms in the UK - and to this day still bears the indelible name of that firm.

All the documents were passed to our solicitor, Ross Wellman at Setfords, now described as a Top 100 Law Firm. To be fair The Twins had provided just about every document needed. The Sale Contract, Lease, Underlease and Management Agreement made up the whole suite required to take any large building and carve it up into little pieces for sale. That`s an insight into the origins of these fractional property sales we`ll come back to.

Ross Wellman is a nice guy and I`d known him for some years. His commercial property experience is enviable and he`s had some top-notch clients. He reviewed all the documents and declared that other than one or two minor amends they were fine and would do the job. He sorted out the amends, topped and tailed them and readied the whole set for sending out to the would-be buyers solicitors.

The Twins said this was a turnkey operation and it was beginning to look like it would be. They would provide everything needed for the meagre fee of just twenty-five thousand pounds. All we needed to do was to find the hotel. Our two new chums would even "manage" it for us for the bargain basement price of ten thousand pounds a month. For that we got a remote "Area Manager" who turned up on one day a week to take the staff out for a beer. In hindsight, we may have seen more activity if we'd stood at the top of Blackpool Tower and thrown ten grand down onto the promenade.

And so off we went. We found a suitable fifty-five bedroomed hotel and agreed to buy it for seven hundred and eighty thousand pounds, with a delayed completion. Fifty-five bedrooms doesn't sound very big but this place was huge. One of the oldest buildings in the centre of Lancaster, it stood five storeys high and another below. It was ridiculously spacious with corridors like motorway carriageways and a dining room with a gallery to grace any Juliet. But what really sticks in my mind is the lift. From the basement to the fifth floor, it travelled without so much as a squeak. Even standing next to it, it was impossible to hear. It clearly wasn't quite as ancient as the property but it was very old. A concertinaed door and a metal trellis style cage encased the whole thing, and it was more in keeping with a hotel in Paris than Dickensian Lancaster.

The hotel was a seriously faded image of a once glorious building. Charles Dickens even stayed there with Wilkie Collins and immortalised it in *The Lazy Tour of Two Idle Apprentices.*

14

Whatever little bit of an entrepreneur there is in me quickly spotted the huge potential. With a little TLC this place could be glorious again.

The Twins lined up the sales team to sell the rooms to investors and we met the boss of RW Invest, Julian Ramsden, firstly at the hotel, the Royal Kings Arms. He brought some of his sales team up from London to check out the hotel before selling it to his clients. He was clearly satisfied that the building existed and wasn't simply a figment of someone's imagination.

We met him for a second time at Dunchurch Park Hotel together with his partner and The Twins. Ramsden was a difficult and generally indifferent young man who seemed anything other than comfortable in his own skin or the workman's boots he seemed to wear all the time. His apparent lack of interpersonal skills didn't help him and confrontation appeared to be his chosen modus operandi which probably explains why we always seemed to be falling out with him.

Nevertheless, RW Invest provided all the marketing material to enable them to sell the rooms, producing a very impressive digital brochure from which even I wouldn't recognise the hotel. Whilst most estate agents charge around one or two percent for their services Ramsden charged us ten percent of all sales fees. Just in case you're wondering, that's not a mistake. Ten percent was their standard charge and Ramsden stood to net around three hundred grand for selling the rooms in this single hotel.

The one item we were asked to provide was a business plan and cashflow forecast for the trading of the hotel. As commercial finance brokers business plans were our forte. We had written plans for just about every type of business over the years and we knew how to interrogate them. The Twins also provided industry standard figures and information. Coupled with family experience in hotels this was the easy part for us. That is, until we looked at what others were doing and became confused by what we saw.

My friend with the two Cheshire hotels, which of course, were also to be managed by The Twins, was selling their rooms at £90K - £100K and provided us with a copy of their forecast for comparison. It didn`t take us more than a few minutes to realise their business forecasts could not possibly sustain such high sale prices and their projects would ultimately fail.

Working out precisely how much a hotel room can return to its owner and therefore be sold at isn`t rocket science. There`s only three hundred and sixty-five days in any one year. Room rates are set, and occupancy rates calculated on known industry levels. These two hotels in Cheshire were both former Travelodge`s and that clearly suggested a lower-end room-rate for, in the main, non-executive types. In other words, budget hotels, budget prices.

At the time of writing (April 2022) one of these two is now an IBIS budget hotel where rooms can be had for as little as forty-five pounds a night – nearly ten years later! Even if the hotel enjoyed one hundred per cent occupancy, which by the way, it will not, its annual revenue for each room would be just over sixteen thousand pounds. According to hotel specialists Knight Frank, average operating profits are thirty-two per cent. In this case that would amount to five thousand two hundred and fifty pounds. That's approximately half of what was promised to investors who purchased rooms for up to one hundred thousand pounds.

But as with most things in life there is a simple answer to why these room sale prices were significantly higher than they should have been. Someone had unilaterally chosen to hike up the figures to bring a higher a return with little or no thought about the consequences. They were, it seems, quite prepared to take the money and run.

Needless to say, the room sale prices at the Royal Kings Arms Hotel were more realistically priced at around half that of the Cheshire pair and approved by The Twins, whatever that meant.

By the time we reached St Georges Day, 23rd April 2014, and with RW Invest marketing the rooms, there was enough cash to complete the purchase. The whole process had taken less than six months. In less than six months we'd gone from busted to booming as the cash rolled in from sales and we now owned a trading hotel to boot.

I like to plan, and we wanted to ensure this new project was well managed. We had relinquished our old football-field-of-an-office and now leased something a whole lot smaller but manageable. One single, open office sufficient to house half a dozen people and desks comfortably. The first-floor space sat on the edge of the runway at Blackpool Airport. Out of the windows we had panoramic views across the sandhills and sea to the west, the whole of the airfield towards St Annes Old Links Golf Course in the south, and the Lake District to the far north. The airport afforded its moments of distraction too, as aeroplanes over-ran the runway or stopped in the middle of it to eject passengers, emergency style. And there was always the Red Arrows on air-show weekends.

After years of contending with the gloom of the credit crunch things were finally looking up.

Within six months of purchasing the hotel RW Invest had sold more than seventy-five per cent of the fifty-five rooms. We planned and started various renovations and improvements at the hotel and were actively busy again and employing our strategy of improving it. The Twins, our so-called management team, were really happy with what had been achieved and no doubt busy spending their ten grand each month. How much was added to that by way of commission from RW Invest we'll probably never know. They were so happy they wanted us to acquire another hotel and began making appointments for us, now at serious hotels with big brand names and even bigger price tags of three or four million. Their cavalier, lets-buy-another-one-this-week attitude clearly carried little or no risk for them. It was all about just two things; building their hotel

18

management brand, Signature Management Services beyond the two properties they already had, and cash. It wasn't difficult to see that if they had five or ten hotels under management each bringing in ten grand a month that would be a lucrative and saleable commodity.

Unfortunately, The Twins had about as much foresight as the films' main character Vince. His mistake of stealing a car containing a valuable machine almost cost him his life. Our two chums could easily have caused us all to end up in jail as what they clearly hadn't foreseen was the intervention of the Financial Conduct Authority (FCA).

In November of 2014 a letter was received from the FCA saying that they were concerned we may be running an unregulated collective investment scheme in breach of various regulations. There's a whole section of law contained in the Financial Services and Markets Act 2000 (FSMA) relating to these schemes. It's lengthy and can easily put you to sleep. Fortunately, the FCA have a way of explaining it in much more succinct manner.

They pointed out that schemes involving the sale of hotel rooms can fall within the provisions of the act and that establishing, operating or winding up such a scheme could amount to a breach. They also pointed out that it is a criminal offence to breach those sections. And as if that's not bad enough they also told us that the promotion of these schemes is also a criminal offence.

What the hell do we do now was all I could think.

The first thing was to give the letter to our management team who dismissed it. It's not a collective they said. Then to RW Invest as they were promoting the scheme. It's not a collective, they said. And then to our own lawyer at Setfords. It's not a collective, he said. All of which was odd as the FCA had very clear views that it was.

We needed to act fast and decisively to show the FCA that we would deal with this professionally. And they had only given us two weeks in which to respond.

Fortunately, I was then introduced to Mike Stubbs, a partner at the renowned law firm Mishcon de Reya, notable amongst other things for having acted for Princess Diana. I've never quite seen a firm spring into action like they did. Mike assembled his team and I recall sitting in a boardroom at Summit House on Red Lion Square in London with about four other partners in the firm for what seemed like a very long time, whilst they set about sorting it out and presenting a solution to restructure the scheme into one that was fully compliant.

In doing so, it became clear that the Magic Circle law firm which drafted the initial documentation got it wrong and The Twins were merely peddling an unlawful scheme. We would never know just how many others they had arranged in this way.

Mishcon de Reya responded quickly to the FCA providing details of a proposed compliant restructure which by now was already underway. Thankfully the FCA confirmed that they were comfortable with the proposals put forward and that no further action would be taken.

On the face of it these transactions appear to be simple property deals with a title fully registered at the UK Land Registry. What could possibly be wrong with that? Particularly as a solicitor will act for all the buyers and should be expected to undertake due diligence on behalf of their clients.

But thousands of investors in the UK and abroad are being lured into parting with their hard-earned cash by promises of high-level returns for these so-called low risk property investments. Meanwhile, hundreds of millions of pounds are being quietly siphoned away by the unlawful operators.

The developers appear to have little or no real knowledge that what they are doing is wrong, whilst some clearly exploit the regulations to the full; the solicitors were completely ignorant of the law, despite warnings from their governing body; the marketing agents simply don`t care as long as they receive their commission. All of which just leaves the investor, that man or woman who has just parted with their life savings, probably in search of a safe haven with better returns than the banks are offering and is now left holding an asset that no-one actually wants because its worthless. Even worse, it's a liability!

In recent years these types of schemes have proliferated the investment sales markets and billions of Pounds, Dollars,

Deutschmark and Yuan have passed through the hands of greedy agents and negligent lawyers into the bank accounts of unscrupulous developers, many of them in offshore jurisdictions.

With the hotel now being owned and managed professionally by corporate services provider Wilton Group we no longer had anything to do with it. But I couldn`t get the idea out of my mind. Surely there`s got to be a way to do this in a compliant manner. As a former legal executive reading legislation was normal and I began to delve more deeply into every bit of it.

Over the next five years I looked at every possible angle. My head was buried deep in the law. I examined what made up these unregulated collective investment schemes, who they could be sold to, and how the sale can be communicated. Every piece of relevant legislation was printed off and formed a significant pile on my desk in the office. I even looked at the twenty-one "Exemptions" provided by the act to see what might be constructed to fit into one of them. At the same time, we kept a very close watch on the marketplace and what was happening.

It was an afternoon in the late summer of 2019 when I finally woke up. By now I can quote chapter and verse of the regulations and had broken them down into easy, bite sized chunks that anyone else could also understand. I know each grain, line and blemish of my desk, the ceiling, and the vast airfield that sits outside our windows from starring out into space whilst thinking through the law and possibilities. I leaned back in my chair and clasped both hands behind my head. "It can't be done," I said out loud, "You can't do this in a compliant manner. It's simply not possible." I had finally realised that the law had been written as a catch-all to drive everyone towards regulation and couldn't be circumvented.

That's when the real fun began.

What I had learned over the preceding five years or so told me that everyone out there doing what we did had also got it wrong. It was also likely that many of those schemes would fail completely due to the unscrupulous methods adopted by some. It was time to tell the world.

In just one afternoon we put together a website to inform people and help those who had sustained losses. That ultimately became UCIS Helpline. In a little over two years, we helped thousands of investors identify whether or not the little piece of property they had purchased in some corner of a foreign field that is forever England was actually a UCIS and concealed merely loss and liability. Our efforts enabled hundreds of those investors to link with specialist lawyers who could and are now helping them to recover their losses.

We continued to monitor the marketplace in the expectation that all these schemes would ultimately fail. We watched with interest the rise of Northern Powerhouse Developments and knew, even when they were recruiting high calibre board members with impressive backgrounds and who really should have known better, that they were operating unregulated collective investment schemes. We knew that Lawrence Kenwright's Signature Living brand was in trouble at least two years before it went into administration because investors were not being paid and were issuing proceedings in the Small Claims Court against his companies. We saw the rise of Shepherd Cox following their acquisition of two hotels in Cheshire from our friend Mike. And we were even called on to educate the wealthy lender who enabled them to buy those properties. He was concerned he might not get his loans back, particularly if the FCA stepped in and closed the hotels down.

Put simply, unregulated property schemes like these were failing almost every day. The extent of this illegal marketplace was staggering. The Hit List at UCIS Helpline has more than three hundred individual hotels, care homes and blocks of student accommodation listed on it. Thousands more investors have been written to and more recovery programmes are being put in place.

But these unlawful schemes continue to be marketed by dishonest developers and their sales teams. However, the story doesn't end there as there are equally dishonest lawyers, lenders and litigation funders who are willing to perpetuate the market and fill their boots with ill-gotten gains.

Over the coming pages I will examine every part of the process to reveal how these unlawful sales have been carried out and warn investors of the pitfalls of buying into an unregulated collective investment scheme. I will expose the wolves in this marketplace for their greed and the duplicitous for their lies including those who have done their best to prevent us from helping all those investors whose lives have been blighted by the Great British Property Scam.

CHAPTER 2

Necessity, The Mother of All Scams

It may now seem like a distant memory, but The Great British Property Scam has many of its roots in the financial crisis of 2008.

When Lehman Brothers filed for bankruptcy on September 15, 2008, hundreds of employees, mostly dressed in business suits, left the bank's offices one by one, carrying their careers in cardboard boxes. Television screens around the world flashed up images of angry staff walking out of expensive office buildings with little to show for their commitment and no idea of what the future held for them.

It was a sombre reminder that nothing lasts forever even in the wealthy financial and investment world, but it was merely the earthquake that caused the tsunami, and few, if any, saw it was coming.

In the days and weeks that followed, other banks went down the same slippery slope into administration, bankruptcy or if they were fortunate, takeover. The result saw the beginning of the worst credit crunch since The Great Depression of the 1930's. This time it was all about property and how great swathes of it had been over valued by so called experts.

Banks and lenders quickly drew in their horns. Lending products disappeared from brokers screens and borrowing criteria was stringently reviewed. Those individual reviews by every recognised lender tightened the criteria to such a degree that it became almost impossible to be approved for a loan. The banks had simply pulled down the shutters while continuing to tell the world at large that they were still open for business.

This resulted in virtually no lending and therefore no dealing in property. No building or developing. Renovations and new build projects remained unfinished or half built. Plots of development land rarely saw the sharp end of a spade. The property industry was brought to its knees.

However, it is an industry that doesn't only employ bricklayers and builders. It is supported by architects, surveyors, solicitor's, lenders, estate agents and brokers. The staff exit from each of those sectors was as busy as that at Lehman Brothers. One small commercial finance broker said that at the time of the crisis they had around £100m of deals they were working on and that were previously capable of being financed. Not a single deal was completed due to the withdrawal of bank funding.

All those professionals needed to work. They needed to feed families and pay mortgages. The mass exodus from the relative safety of professional life therefore produced another driving force in the development of these new scams as some of the

27

more adventurous individuals were prepared to take greater risks.

The legal sector was hit particularly hard. With impending legislation already threatening to all but wipe out the claim's arena, a lucrative area of work for lawyers, large numbers of the profession were desperately trying to find alternative work.

Necessity and creativity, however, will often produce a result, particularly when opportunity comes knocking. It did for a relatively small number of law firms. These pliable lawyers went on to make a name for themselves within a murky pool of developers who were selling hotel rooms, student pods and care homes. The vast majority were unregulated collective investment schemes (UCIS).

The Solicitors Regulation Authority (SRA) has carried advice and warnings about solicitor's involvement in Collective Investment Schemes since at least 2013. The SRA say:

> "We have warned for a number of years about the risks posed by dubious or questionable investment schemes.........Schemes are being promoted as involved in the routine buying of a property when in reality the buyer's money is being used to finance a high-risk development or refurbishment. This is of particular concern in unusual developments such as the buying of individual hotel rooms, rooms in care homes, or self-storage units.........We are seeing cases of solicitors simply processing transactions for buyers

while adopting the language of conveyancing. The effect is to mask what is really happening.............The Serious Fraud Office have previously investigated losses of up to £120m arising from the promotion of self-storage schemes................Many of these schemes are likely to be "collective investment schemes" under section 235 of the Financial Services and Markets Act 2000. If those involved in the schemes are not authorised by FCA, they will be committing a criminal offence and are likely to be imprisoned."

Unfortunately, those high-risk firms of solicitors chose to ignore the advice of their regulator and continue processing these types of transactions. Some created conveyancing factories doing nothing else but acting on the purchase of these schemes. One particular lawyer, a partner in his Yorkshire based firm was heard to say to a proposed developer, "I don`t care if you`re selling a collective investment scheme as you`ll go to jail not me."

Whilst there are lawyers around who will process these transactions the unscrupulous developers will seek them out. Even as this is being written there are UCIS`s being marketed and sold to unwary investors with the help of sales agents and UK law firms.

Coincidentally, all this was happening at the same time another equally creative scam was being touted to unwary investors.

Between 2005 and 2010 Countrywide Land Holdings unlawfully sold minute, worthless plots of land to UK investors with the promise of high-level gains from future Planning Permissions.

Land banking companies divide land into smaller plots, often only a single square foot, to sell to investors, with the expectation it will soar in value once it's available for development. However, the land is often in areas of natural beauty or historical interest, with little chance of it being built on. Investors are told they will make money on small plots of land once planning permission is granted or development started. Permission is often not granted or even applied for, and investors are left with land that is practically worthless. It is often not made clear to investors that there are restrictions on the development of the land or that it is protected.

Countrywide Land Holdings netted c£33m in the process of selling small plots to unwary investors and the Financial Conduct Authority (FCA) have only been able to recover £2.5m to distribute amongst them. The scheme was deemed to have been an unregulated collective investment scheme.

The Land Banking scam was now upon us and would be repeated by many other so-called developers, many of which have been jailed. As a result, considerable losses have been recorded by investors in these schemes. Many British companies offering plots of land have failed or been shut down by the Financial Conduct Authority and directors of some of those companies were jailed.

In one instance a solicitor was one of eight men convicted of fraud, which to date has led to sentences totalling 26 years' immediate imprisonment.

According to Legal Futures, between July 2008 and November 2011, the group ran three companies – Plott Investments Ltd, which changed its name to Plott UK Ltd, European Property Investments (UK) Ltd, and Stirling Alexander Ltd.

Salesmen for the companies cold-called potential investors to sell them agricultural land that the companies had bought for minimal amounts, as well as land the companies did not own. Using sales scripts, misleading promotional material, and high-pressure sales techniques, they lied about the current and future value of the land.

People were persuaded to purchase land at vastly inflated prices, on the false promise of a substantial profit. The scheme extracted at least £4.3m from 110 investors and none of them have seen a return from what was also deemed an unregulated collective investment scheme.

The seed was sown. The growth in property development would now come in fractionalisation, the break-up of larger property into smaller units, and advance sales. The alternative investment market was primed and marketing terms like "arm's length," "hands off," and "armchair investments" all became commonplace in brochures advertising fractional property sales.

However, what really started the fire began back in 2004.

On Friday May 7th, 2004, Country Life magazine reported that a new hotel in Notting Hill was to offer guests the opportunity to save on hotel bills when staying in London, as well as a getting good rate of return on a new kind of investment.

Guesthouse West was described as "a brand-new venture aiming to be a luxurious modern hotel providing a quiet atmosphere for people staying there, as well as good accessibility to all the attractions the capital has to offer…..The hotel is also an investment opportunity for businessmen or companies who are looking to save on hotel costs for those staying the night as well as a return on investment."

A totally new concept was born and anyone with sufficient cash could buy into it. Rooms in the hotel were for sale on a 99-year lease at prices that started at £235,000. Investors would get "up to" a 7% return on their investment by allowing the hotel to let the room out for them. With hotel room prices in London always coming at a premium this may have been an attractive proposition for some. Particularly with GuestInvest's high profile advertising campaign promising investors that they could; "Earn money while others sleep."

Unfortunately, as was seen with Lehman Brothers, all good things come to an end and by 2008 the headlines were very different. On Friday October 3rd it was announced that the company who introduced the concept of "buy-to-let" hotel rooms had fallen into administration. But not before leaving its mark across London and the investment sector.

GuestInvest owned Blakes Hotel in London's Mayfair, patronised by celebrities such as Robert de Niro, Gwyneth Paltrow, and Diana Ross, and was developing a string of other hotels, including one on the site of the former Whitbread Brewery in the City of London. Hundreds of investors paid upwards of £250,000 for a GuestInvest hotel room. In 2007 they bought Blakes from the former actress Anouska Hempel for about £34m. The rooms at Blakes were on sale for £1m each.

In September 2006, GuestInvest's founder, Johnny Sandelson, entered into a £140m joint venture with HBOS to finance new hotel acquisitions, and brought in financier Sir Mark Weinberg, Life President of St James's Place Wealth Management and husband of Anouska Hempel, as a non-executive director. Arguably, both should have recognised that the GuestInvest model was going to fail.

Many investors blamed GuestInvest for overspending on acquisitions and development projects. At the time of the collapse one hotel industry investment expert said: "They probably paid far too much for the assets they bought, and they spent an awful lot of money (renovating them), going way over budget."

In an interview with The Observer, Sandelson said: "Everybody seems to love the concept of owning a hotel room. It makes good financial sense - investors get good returns and a bit of usage as well as capital growth. So, it's a very strong proposition and people seem to warm to it."

With those who parted with up to £400,000 for a GuestInvest buy-to-let hotel room suffering sleepless nights, any suggested warmth has more than diminished.

According to industry specialist CBRE in Aug 2020 hotels have historically averaged a Gross Operating Profit margin of 11.6 percent. How does that equate to the GuestInvest financials?

Available room nights:		365
Occupancy Levels:		85%
Average Room Rate Blakes Hotel in 2021:		£270
Total Room Revenue for year:		£83,767
Hotel Room Profit:	x11.6%	£9717
Investor Purchase Price:	£250,000 x 7% = £17,500 (promised return)	

You don`t need to be the President of a distinguished wealth management firm to work out that the figures don`t add up. It is equally concerning that whilst we have not been able to examine the scheme documents for GuestInvest it clearly had all the hallmarks of an unregulated collective investment scheme. Investors were sold "property" which was then

34

"managed" for them by the developer or hotel management company. We will examine later the legal make-up of a Collective Investment Scheme.

Jointly, GuestInvest and Countrywide Land Holdings had revealed that fractionalised property sales could generate huge amounts of money. It was now time for the scams to move into the provinces where the financial dynamics were very different.

If those professionals mentioned above all support the property development arena it`s the developers who create it. Without developers the support acts wouldn`t exist. As the tsunami in 2008 gathered ground the developers either went out of business, hibernated until the economic climate improved or became more "creative" in their approach to funding methods. Sadly, it`s that latter group who were responsible for what has become The Great British Property Scam.

As the financial collapse of 2008 took hold the unscrupulous developers saw that it was easier to break up a property, sell it piecemeal and make a lot more profit in doing so. As a result, a glut of allegedly appealing investments in car parking spaces, storage units, student accommodation blocks, hotels and more recently care homes hit the market. They all carried promises of glittering annual returns which were in many cases totally unachievable, and the investments are completely unsaleable by their owners.

In early 2021 a nationally recognised firm of business agents valued an investors unit in a block of c500 student accommodation units in Bradford for the purposes of a group claim being made by investors. The unit was described as worthless by the firm. The investor had paid circa £60,000 for it and had ongoing liabilities to pay each year. Not only was the unit worthless it is now a liability due to service charges and ground rents that were payable on them.

On 30 April 2019 the court made an order to wind-up four Store First companies in the public interest by consent between those four companies and the Secretary of State.

The scheme, which sold storage pods to investors, was promoted by former Top Gear presenter Quentin Willson. He appeared in several advertisements endorsing the scheme and unfortunately invested in Store First himself.

Store First offered a starting investment of £3,750 and a maximum of £1 million. Over a thousand individual investors are thought to have been affected by the alleged fraud, including those who invested their pension funds through the Capita Oak Pension and Henley Retirement Benefit schemes along with many individual SIPPS. The amounts invested totalled over £120m. The company guaranteed investors high returns and a buy-back scheme, but these promises were not kept.

The Serious Fraud Office has opened an investigation into the Capita Oak Pension and Henley Retirement Benefit schemes, Self-Invested Personal Pensions (SIPPS) as well as other storage pod investment schemes.

Many developers who saw fractional sales as an easy way to fund a project now find themselves being chased or sued by investors for the return of their purchase monies. The following is a small selection. Where known we have added the approximate number of individual units (rooms) they have developed or sold from information obtained from the Land Registry.

- ALPHA Developments (c2500)
- MBi Qualia Care (700+)
- St Camillus (90+)
- Shepherd Cox (380+)
- Carlauren (650+)
- Dylan Harvey (1000+)
- Elliot Group (5000+)
- Northern Powerhouse Developments (780+)
- D.J. Suites / Daniel Johns (1400+)
- Pinnacle (880+)
- Signature Living

NB. Source: HM Land Registry. Only those rooms which have been registered are enumerated.

Many of these are already in administration. Some are the subject of Group Litigation claims. They have all carried out numerous developments where individual rooms in hotels, care homes and student accommodation have been sold to investors who have now lost money. They form part of a list of around 250 similar developments where a total of 25,000 individual units have been sold. The list is by no means complete as previously unknown developments are regularly coming to the fore.

But that is only one part of the picture. The other was the dramatic drop in interest rates following the collapse of Lehman Brothers and the ensuing credit crisis. Suddenly, all those people who had been prudent with their finances, probably throughout their whole lives, now found that the banks were not offering anything like a decent return on their money. One or two per cent (if they could get it!) wasn`t going to fund their retirements and a whole new marketplace erupted out of the ashes of Lehmans. Investors needed to put their money somewhere and everyone has been told at some time that land and property is a safe bet.

By 2016, it was estimated there were 1.4 million SIPPs in the UK, totalling £175bn in assets. There are now estimated to be around two million in existence and GlobalData projects the market to grow by a further £1.9bn. As we have seen with Store First some of that money has already gone into and been lost in unregulated collective investment schemes.

If a decade of austerity has taken its toll on UK investors it has served those from overseas well. The combined effect of low interest and attractive exchange rates has seen the UK become even more of a target for foreign investors and particularly those from the Far East.

UK property has always been a prime target for overseas investors, but in recent times the number of properties let by non-UK based owners has soared. Property investors from Asia, the US, Europe and more have viewed the UK property market as a solid investment location for many years, with strong capital appreciation, growing rental markets and the support of continued private and public investment across the country.

Now, new data revealed by Hamptons International shows that the number of investors based abroad who let out property in the UK has spiked and is up from 7% to 11% of the total market share.

One major factor influencing overseas investors right now is the depreciation of the sterling since the EU referendum in 2016. Favourable exchange rates for foreign investors mean they get much more for their money now than they once did, opening a wider section of the market. Often, much of that overseas money ends up in developments that are never finished or room investments that will never provide the promised returns.

We will look at this in more detail later but for now it is helpful to look at how The Financial Services and Markets Act 2000 (FSMA) sets out what constitutes a Collective Investment Scheme (CIS).

S235 says that a CIS relates to property of "any" description.....the purpose of which is to enable those taking part to receive profits or income arising from the acquisition;

the investor must not have day-to-day control over the management of the property; the contributions of the investors and the profits or income out of which payments are to be made to them are pooled; and, *or* the property is managed as a whole by or on behalf of the operator of the scheme.

The vast majority of these schemes will be caught by that final "management" clause as most have a single manager appointed by the developer. It's difficult to imagine a 500-space car park or 100 bedroomed hotel being looked after by multiple managers on behalf of numerous investors.

And therein lies the difficulty. As we'll see later, it is almost impossible for these types of schemes to be organised in a compliant manner unless the developer seeks the approval of the FCA. Without that approval these schemes will continue to be not only unregulated but also unlawful.

The good news for investors is that there is the possibility of recovering their losses. It is unlikely to come from the provisions for compensation offered by the legislation because that will require the developer to pay back what they've received. In most cases that will not happen because the developer has already spent the money on lavish lifestyles or allegedly invested it in their next project.

Over the coming pages we will examine all the fault lines in these projects and how all the pieces of the jigsaw come together to create The Great British Property Scam.

CHAPTER 3

Rules of Engagement

Perhaps one of the most striking features about the regulations which control collective investments is that they came into force more than twenty years ago on the 1$^{st\,of}$ December 2001. However, despite the passing of two decades they are still being ignored by lawyers, developers, and their sales agents and the law continues to be broken.

We are of course, all now familiar with the well-established legal principle of ignorance of the law being no excuse. Aristotle translated it as "nemo censetur ignorare legem", meaning "*nobody* is thought to be ignorant of the law". The addition of "nobody" will be important for many of those lawyers, developers, and agents.

The Financial Services and Markets Act 2000 (FSMA) introduced various regulations to protect consumers and control market abuse. It also created the Financial Services Authority (since renamed as the Financial Conduct Authority (FCA)) as a regulator for insurance, investment business and banking. In other words, just about everything financial.

Unfortunately, we can`t ignore the legislation if we are to have clarity on what constitutes a Collective Investment Scheme (CIS). It`s also a fact that legislation is rarely an easy read. It is written by lawyers for lawyers and often comes with the warning that it can seriously damage your state of mind. A quick scan of the contents of the act reveals a very lengthy piece of legislation that is, in essence, no different. The challenge is to take that heavily legalistic language and turn it into understandable English. So let`s try to simplify it.

Section 235 of the act says that collective investment schemes can be any arrangements relating to any type of property, including money. When the BoE FMLC reported in 2008, they said this can be just about anything, even a group of "Ostriches". Clearly, the use of one very small word, "any", opens up collective investment schemes way beyond the unusual and takes us into everyday territory.

However, it is necessary to understand what the purpose or effect of any such scheme is. According to the act it must enable those taking part to receive profits or income from the acquisition, holding, management or disposal of the property. In other words, the arrangement must cause you to profit from it. Why else would you be in it if not for profit.

Additionally, in order to be considered a collective investment scheme the owners of the individual rooms or units must not have day-to-day control over the management of the property, even if they have the right to be consulted.

So, up to now we have "any" type of property, which must provide a profit and the buyer should not have day-to-day control. So far so good. There are just two more things to consider in order to know whether the arrangement amounts to a collective investment scheme.

Firstly, will the money paid by the buyers to acquire their units, or any of the income or profit generated by the property go into a single pool. Secondly, is the property managed as a whole by the operator of the scheme (or someone appointed by them). In order to qualify as a collective one or both of these two characteristics must be present.

Many schemes are caught on the pooling of income but even where that isn`t happening the management of the property is problematic for a great many of these schemes. It is, after all, impossible to see how a hotel, care home or student accommodation block with, say, a hundred rooms could be looked after by multiple managers.

To recap, an arrangement relating to any type of property where the investor is getting a profit, doesn`t have day-to-day control, and monies or management are being pooled is almost certainly a collective investment scheme. If it`s not registered with the Financial Conduct Authority, it automatically becomes an unregulated scheme or UCIS.

In the midst of simplifying what could have been a nauseating read there are five words or phrases which need to be expounded a little further, if only to show that full consideration has been given. They are, arrangements, day-to-day control, pooling, management as a whole, and operator.

Arrangements:

In a report in 2008 The Bank of England Financial Markets Law Committee (FMLC) acknowledged that the scope of this definition is clearly "very wide". It is also clear that the arrangements may apply to "property of *any* description" and are not restricted to "investments". A CIS can relate to, for example, real estate, rights under betting contracts or even to ostriches they say.

The renowned legal counsel, John Virgo agreed, saying, "The term "arrangements" is very wide in scope. In particular, no formality is required and there is no requirement for any legally enforceable agreements."

The wording used in the legislation is broad enough to cover all stages of a transaction, from the preparatory step of gathering in funds up to and including the making of the communal investment. Therefore, the fact that an investor's funds may rest in client account pending putting in place a particular loan, does not stop it being in a CIS. If the money was placed there for the purpose of such an arrangement, it is from that time in a CIS.

The FMLC also noted that "there is no need for the participants to have any ownership or other interest in the property, or to receive directly the profits or income arising from its management" to be caught by the regulations.

"Arrangements" can also fall within the scope of the act if their "purpose" is to enable those taking part to participate in the relevant profits or income, even if this is not achieved; and conversely where this is the "effect" of the arrangements, even if this is not their purpose, or primary purpose.

The FCA have said that they will always "look through" arrangements to see what the original intention was as well as strictly enforcing the legislation. The FCA Perimeter Guidance in PERG 11 indicates that 'if a scheme, in substance, is a collective investment scheme, it cannot escape the need for regulation by being dressed up as something else.' This view was endorsed in FCA v Capital Alternatives in that the reference to the "purpose or effect" of the arrangements reflected the fact that what mattered was the way in which the scheme was run in practice and not contractual terms which might not reflect reality.

The FMLC report of 2008 states that "the breadth of the definition (of "arrangements") is clearly intentional, and the aim is to cast the regulatory net wide". Developers or operators are therefore left with either seeking regulatory approval of their project or relying on the twenty-one exclusions contained in the act, which are unlikely to help them. (We will look at those exclusions later).

"Property of any description" clearly, therefore, includes the likes of hotel rooms, student accommodation units, rooms in care homes, storage units and even the ill-fated car parking spaces. There appears no doubt that all of the property types referred to in these pages fit within the definition of "arrangements" but that many others will also fall within the scope of the legislation.

Day-to-day control

One of the features of most of the UCIS sales that have been made to ordinary investors is that they are "fully managed". The phrases "armchair investment" and "arms-length investment" have also been used frequently to describe a supposedly hassle-free arrangement. The investor merely has to pay over his money, sit back and await the promised monthly returns.

The FMLC thought the notion of "day to day control" vague and the act does not give any further guidance on how it should be interpreted. Furthermore, the phrase "whether or not they have the right to be consulted or to give directions", which purports to clarify the "day to day control of the property" notion, is also obscure. There is no clear picture as to what level of control the "right to be consulted or to give directions" refers to.

The 2008 report says, "Day-to-day control over the management of..." is not a wholly easy concept. "Control over the management of..." is presumably intended to be distinguished from "management of..." i.e., arrangements will not qualify simply because the participants do not manage the property themselves. On the other hand, "day to day control" must clearly mean more than having the "right to be consulted or to give directions". In Elliott, Laddie J referred "in colloquial terms" to "minding the shop". In practice it is not always easy to apply the test, though it appears that as a minimum the participants should be in a position to tell the person who is actually managing the property what to do on a continuing day-to-day basis."

John Virgo said, "Given the relevance of day-to-day control in determining the question of whether a CIS exists or not, the common-sense view must be that an "operator" is most likely to be the person to whom day-to-day control has been conferred.

In the Capital Alternatives case it was concluded that whether there was day-to-day control depended on whether such control was actually exercised not on whether investors had a contractual right to exercise it.

In practice it seems wholly illogical that, say, one hundred bedrooms in a single hotel could all be managed individually by their owners, the investors. Similarly, units in a block of student accommodation or care home, storage unit or car park, would be almost impossible to manage individually. Since all or most of these schemes have a "management company" set up by the operator the requirement that the participants do not have day-to-day control seems easily met.

Pooling:

Interestingly, while some developers and operators get hung up on this clause, probably in their efforts to explain why they are not pooling income and/or profits, the FMLC said that this clause "does not seem to give any particular problems". As a result, they did not consider the point further in their thirty-four-page report.

It is, however, difficult to understand how pooling isn`t present in all those arrangements which provide alleged "guaranteed returns". No two hotel rooms or car parking spaces, etc. are going to enjoy the same level of occupation – despite what our old friend Mr Ten Per Cent had everyone believe – that they operated a fair rotation of rooms given out to guests - try telling one of your best customers that they can`t have their favourite room again and see the response!

Management as a whole:

This criterion, and the contrast with the alternative of "pooling", makes it clear that arrangements can (in the absence of an exclusion) amount to a CIS even though each participant is entitled to a distinct part of the property if all such property is "managed as a whole". Take the example of an asset manager who provides a "managed fund service", i.e., buys and sells units in investment funds for its clients on the basis of pre-set models depending on the client's risk appetite: all clients with the same risk appetite will hold investments of the same kind in the same proportions, even though these may be held in separate accounts beneficially owned by the individual clients.

49

It is arguable that notwithstanding the distinct entitlements the "arrangements" under which they are managed may fall within the CIS definition. This view is supported by the existence of a partial exclusion within the Act for "individual investment management assignments".

In *FCA v Capital Alternatives* ......Whether in considering if the 'property' was 'managed as a whole' one looked at the generation of profits specific to a plot or took a broad view as to physical acts of management Christopher Clarke LJ said: 'The phrase "the property is managed as a whole" uses words of ordinary language. I do not regard it as appropriate to attach to the words some form of exclusionary test based on whether the elements of individual management were "substantial" - an adjective of some elasticity. The critical question is whether a characteristic feature of the arrangements under the scheme is that the property to which those arrangements relate is managed as a whole. Whether that condition is satisfied requires an overall assessment and evaluation of the relevant facts. For that purpose, it is necessary to identify (i) what is "the property", and (ii) what is the management thereof which is directed towards achieving the contemplated income or profit. It is not necessary that there should be no individual management activity - only that the nature of the scheme is that, in essence, the property is managed as a whole, to which question the amount of individual management of the property will plainly be relevant'.

Once again, it is hard to see how the likes of an hotel with many bedrooms or any of the other asset classes frequently referred to within these pages can be managed in any other way than as a whole.

Operator

"Operator" and "operate" are not defined generally in FSMA. Section 237 states that in relation to a unit trust scheme with a separate trustee, "operator" means the manager and that in relation to an open-ended investment company it means that company.

The key area in practice is whether a) "operation" extends to the overall "running" of the scheme, including the management of its assets (this is understood to be the view of the FCA); or b) is limited to the "administrative" aspects of operation (including, in particular, the accounting and calculations involved in the "collective" nature of the structure) to the exclusion of asset management. The distinction is particularly important in funding structures (particularly limited partnerships) where separate entities perform the asset management and administrative functions. If the view in (a) is correct, both entities may be regarded as "operating" and will need to be authorised under FSMA. On the view in (b), the asset manager will not need authorisation as an "operator" and may not need authorisation at all if the assets concerned are not themselves "investments" within the meaning of the Regulated Activities Order contained within FSMA 2000.

As can be seen, whilst legislation can often be complicated and tedious, here, what constitutes a CIS comes down to a few simple things:

- any arrangements, regarding,
- property of any description,
- enabling people to profit from taking part,
- where they don`t have day-to-day control,
- the contributions, profits or income are pooled, and,
- it`s managed as a whole by the operator.

The chances are that if you`re one of those unfortunate investors who has acquired a hotel room, storage unit, care home room or a student pod you have purchased into an unregulated collective investment scheme.

What many people, even those within the industry don`t realise is that whilst the legislation is written as a catch-all it also provides as many as twenty-one exemptions contained in a schedule to the act referred to as, "Arrangements not amounting to a collective investment scheme". That`s twenty-one opportunities for developers to find a compliant way to do what they do. The full list is included at the end of this book.

CHAPTER 4

Illusionists

The world of sales is sometimes a murky reflection of real life. Frequently, it`s simply a case of somebody who knows someone who can sell this, that, or the other. Sometimes, however, it's a case of making something look very different from what it really is in order to sell it to someone, a bit like "clocking" in the motor trade. But that of course is illegal.

Make no mistake, everything has to be sold and we all sell something, from our time to our abilities. I`ve attended business training courses where there have been ongoing arguments about which discipline should come first, business accounting or business sales. The accountants will always argue that accounting systems must be in place before anything happens in the business in order to log it properly when it does. But one thing is absolutely certain; if there are no sales the accounts system is pointless. Sales are the be-all and end-all of every business!

You can be forgiven for thinking that all property is marketed and/or sold to buyers by professional estate agents. If this were so, there would be some comfort to be taken in the fact that the vast majority of estate agents are now members of The National Association of Estate Agents (NAEA) or better still the Royal Institution of Chartered Surveyors (RICS).

However, many of the agents who operate in this particular area of investment sales have no licence or qualifications whatsoever. They hide behind toothless organisations like The Property Ombudsman, suggesting that this is a regulator when in fact it`s nothing more than a mediation service. Some even suggest that they are "affiliated" to, for instance, the Information Commissioners Office and even Trading Standards when in reality those organisations simply don`t provide for affiliation because both are Regulators. Sales agents are merely using these names to build confidence with potential investors and create an illusion.

They also create that illusion in other ways. In particular, they love to quote credible and reputable sources to hang their sales pitch on. The top estate agents are frequently used to suggest that buying the unit on offer makes sense. The likes of Knight Frank and Savills, both of which produce regular market reports, will often be quoted, sometimes out of context to support the sales in a development – as we`ll see again shortly.

Furthermore, they don`t necessarily consider themselves to be lowly "estate agents" but Property Investment Agents. It is, after all, a much more impressive title and one which conjures up a degree of professionalism. But ultimately, they`re all salespeople, many of whom have no professional training in selling property. And yet they are selling "investments", often to people who don`t qualify as High Net Worth or Sophisticated Investors as required by the legislation. If, as an investor you are uncertain about the statutory requirements you will find the relevant forms in the appendices at the back of this book.

One of the most well-known and long-standing agents is Knight Knox, whose home page says, "Property investment made simple". They state clearly that they are selling investments. Over the last 20 years, they say their sales are valued at more than £1.2B.

Another prominent agent is our old friend RW Invest. At the date of writing, their website claims, *"Thanks to our unrivalled investment opportunities, award-winning team, and five-star customer service, we've helped over 75,000 people achieve their investment goals."* If their claim is true, then that would amount to sales of circa £3.75B (using £50K as an average sale). Their usual commission rate is 10% and that would return them £375m. You might expect Julian Ramsden to be wearing something other than those builder`s boots he had a liking for. On the other hand, of course, you may take the view that their claims are less than wholly accurate.

Another agent is One Touch Property Investment. Their claim is similar, *"One Touch is your first point of contact for property investment in the UK"*. They offer student accommodation, hotel rooms and care home rooms and yet still claim to be "Your partner in prosperity". Again, at the date of writing their site states that they have had 1758 "properties acquired". If we are to assume that what they really mean is 1758 properties sold to investors, then that would equate to £87.9m in sales and £8.79m in fee income.

Already, we can see that there is a lot of money being made in this industry. That might seem perfectly acceptable, particularly to anyone with a background in business, until we look deeper to see where that money is being extracted from. We`ll come back to this in the section about developers.

The name Armchair Invest appears a great many times on our Hit List. Their website says, *"Armchair Invest Limited is a leading provider of the best investment opportunities across the UK"*. Nothing unclear about "investment opportunities." They go on to say, *"We have been in the property investment business for numerous years and undertake comprehensive due diligence to ensure all client purchases are safe and secure"*. And yet they continue to offer investments in some of the most unsecure forms such as car parking spaces which were outlawed by the FCA in 2019. Similarly, Armchair Invest currently offer units in the student accommodation development at Granite House Liverpool. For this purpose, they quote the renowned and highly reputable estate agent Knight Frank by reference to a report carried out by that firm in 2016. *"According to research carried out by Knight Frank in 2016 some £3.1 billion was invested in purpose-built student accommodation, which is more than double the level of investment seen in 2013 and 2014*

- a clear indication that there is a market for this type of property."

At this point it is perhaps worth reminding ourselves that according to the legislation collective investment schemes are classified as *any* arrangements, regarding *property* of *any* description. Remember those Ostriches!

However, it also needs noting that not all property purchases are unlawful. Buying a house as an investment to let out in flats is perfectly legal. You could buy a whole block of flats and let them out to tenants without breaking any laws.

Before we look further at other examples of agents selling these unlawful products it`s confession time again. I don`t admit this to many people and certainly not in good establishments that I have no desire to be thrown out of, but......I used to be an estate agent. Yes, OK, I can here the groans and feel the arrows.

It was nearly forty years ago when I decided to leave the law firm I was with – somewhat sooner than they wanted me to – and set up my own agency. I`d worked for another agency for a while, had my legal experience and my wife`s knowledge of mortgages whilst employed for the largest building society in the UK. But we sold ordinary, everyday, homes. Domestic property, the whole of which was being sold by one person to another. The real point of mentioning this is that I know that you don`t have to be the brain of Britain to be an estate agent. Some may have tried to wax lyrical about the skills involved but the reality is that sale boards sell houses, or at least they did back then. These days, the internet can do a much better job.

The point of this confession was highlighted to me during a recent conversation with an investor. She told me that having received an unexpected email warning her that the investment she had made into a block of student accommodation was likely to be a UCIS, she had called the developer's office to discuss it. The girl at the other end of the phone said that she had never heard of unregulated collective investment schemes before, but they could still sell her unit for her. In other words, they could help her to commit an offence. Its clear that the developer's office had no understanding of the regulations or the constraints and repercussions of contravening them.

Over the last seven or eight years I have met with a number of the people running these sales agencies. A few are seemingly nice guys trying to act as professionally as their experience and knowledge allow and will certainly do their best to achieve sales for a would-be developer. This does, of course, raise an immediate question about where their allegiances lie and who these agents are really acting for.

Almost all of the websites for these agents state that they undertake extensive due diligence on the investments they sell, are there to assist their "clients" in making the right purchase and they will go to the moon and back to ensure their "clients" get the best possible deal – a deal that's right for them. I suppose it doesn't seem unreasonable that if an agent finds someone who buys one unit from him, he wants to hold on to him and sell him another. That's simply the nature of the beast. However, with an average unit sale currently appearing to be at least £60K the agent is on circa £6k for every sale – paid to them by the developer.

It's worth remembering the story of The Twins. They introduced RW Invest to us, just as they had done previously on other developments they had been involved with. Compare this with selling your own home. You, as the homeowner choose your estate agent and enter into an agreement with them for their fees, payable on completion of the sale. The estate agent is, at all times, acting for you, their client, because you are responsible for paying their fees. The same is true in the investment sales market because the developer is always on the hook for the agent's fees. Now imagine a situation where you've decided to sell your home but before you put it on the market with an estate agent you're approached by a total stranger saying they want to buy your home and have their own estate agent who will value it for you – or should that be them?

There is also the issue of what the agent may charge the buyer for the alleged privilege of buying a property they are marketing. Many agents have done this even though it creates the further illusion of the buyer being a client of the agent. The essence of agency is that one party (the agent) facilitates contracts between a principal and a third party on the principal's behalf. Typically, the agent receives a commission from the principal for his or her efforts.

When agents assist buyers or sellers they get a commission. For that reason, they assume legal responsibilities. If they make mistakes, hide information or misrepresent clients, they could be liable to pay a compensation in relation to the damages suffered by the clients.

One of the first salespeople I had some contact with was Stuart Gibbons at Investinrooms. The very name itself is a giveaway. I recall clearly being told by him that as well as running his business he also undertook work for the FCA. At the time of writing his website says, "Investinrooms provides transparent and sustainable property investments". The site goes on to quote;

It was back in 2012 with our sister company Millbak Wealth, who were SIPP compliant, dealing in Loan Notes & Bonds for HNW's with funds allocated from pension funds, that we decided we wanted to offer investment property opportunities, based on Buy2Lets directly to investors. Investinrooms was born.

In this way clients could own a property on a long lease, registered at land registry and handled by a regulated solicitor acting on behalf of the investor.

*Over the last 8 years we have added Hotels and Student Accommodation to the Investinrooms **portfolio.** These have proven very popular with investors and are deemed to be commercial property and so are taxed very differently from*

61

buying an apartment or flat. In the vast majority of
*cases **income is tax free.***

The process generally includes two set of solicitors provided for
the sales and purchase process. As a result the compliance
process is as good as can be provided. Occasionally for further
clarification Barristers are consulted.

All transactions are conducted through UK solicitors. Leases
are issued to investors and buy back agreements/options form
part of the legal sales contract.

How can an investor receive a return that benefits them? We
ALL know property is the key. But buying a house, renovating,
dealing with builders, architects, planners and then tenants can
all be a nightmare.

Will the house go up in value or could it go down? Do I need a
mortgage and what about the legal costs and stamp duty? And
what could you purchase for under, say £80,000, even if you
could get the money.

You can be forgiven for thinking that Investinrooms is trying
to dissuade you from purchasing an ordinary property, say, a
house or an apartment, both of which would be perfectly legal
of course. But statements like those above are clearly going to
make people believe that investing in a room is a sensible thing
to do – something the FCA clearly don`t agree with and The
Solicitors Regulations Authority warns its members about. It`s
also worth mentioning that it`s now two or three years since my

last conversation with Stuart Gibbons and others he works with. At that time, I told him very clearly that what he was selling were unregulated collective investment schemes.

Operationally, these sales firms work in various ways. Most will have a bank of sub-agents in the UK and around the world. Many of these are individuals marketing to a group of close associates or to another agency. The well-established agents will always look to have a sole arrangement with the developer in order that they can control who sells what.

Many agents here in the UK generally operate with a sales team of their own working in-house, but still being self-employed and paid only on results – meaning that they must sell in order to earn a living. These teams can be of any size from five or six up to a dozen or more. The agents rely on generating leads from their website and each agent would be given a particular number of these leads at the start of the week. This might be added to daily if the website is doing its job.

This creates teams of salespeople, all working together under the same roof, bouncing off each other by way of incentive and encouragement. Sales will be recorded and noted openly for all to see. Additional rewards are also provided to those outstanding individuals, and this can be anything from a bottle of expensive Champagne to a weekend at the Ritz. It's all about encouraging sales.

Each individual will also have different methods they use to make a sale. All will constantly ask for sales incentives for the buyer, no legal fees or a price reduction for "today only". But the most highly sought-after skill is that of "switching". If an enquirer can be switched from the product they're really interested in to the product the agency wants to sell to them, that salesperson can generally name his own price.

There is, as always, a reason for this skill to be so highly prized, as witnessed at RW Invest. The ability to switch a buyer to something else enables the agency to advertise property they don't actually have and doesn't even exist. This enables them to use the likes of Rightmove to advertise that fictitious property.

It has to be said that Rightmove would not normally allow agents to advertise, for instance, a hotel room for sale. However, if the agency creates a false image of, say, a small apartment, using a postcode close to that of the hotel room, when a potential buyer calls about that advertisement, they can be switched on to the hotel room.

But of course, all this conjures up an image of a sales force operating in a manner inconsistent with openness and honesty. You might in fact think of these sales teams as little more than "Boiler Rooms." So let's take a moment to look at precisely what a "Boiler Room" is, in this context.

As this is potentially very important, we want to ensure that our point of reference is strong. Let's start with the investment site Investopedia. It describes a boiler room as "a place or operation—usually a call centre—where high-pressure salespeople call lists of potential investors ("sucker lists") to peddle speculative, sometimes fraudulent, securities." It also says, "A broker using boiler-room tactics gives customers only positive information about the stock and discourages them from doing any outside research. Boiler room salespeople typically use catchphrases like "it's a sure thing" or "opportunities like this happen once in a lifetime." Sounding familiar yet?

Part of the pressure sales approach may include making assertions about the investment opportunity that the target cannot verify on their own because no legal documentation is available to be inspected by the buyer prior to paying a substantial deposit to secure the unit. Promises of high returns and no risk might also be used to pressure prospects to invest.

According to Investopedia Boiler-room tactics are sometimes used to convince investors to overspend on the purchase of securities that are actually of lower value. The securities may, in fact, be worthless or non-existent, and the funds that are raised are solely for the enrichment of the individuals behind the operation. This goes to value of the units being sold and we'll also come back to later.

Action Fraud is the UK's national reporting centre for fraud and cybercrime. It provides a central point of contact for information about fraud and financially motivated internet crime and is run by the City of London Police working alongside the National Fraud Intelligence Bureau (NFIB). It says, "The majority of investment frauds are run out of offices known as **boiler rooms.**".

Fraud implies knowledge. Or does it? We already know that being ignorant of the law provides no excuse for breaking it. But what is "fraud" apart from a widely used term that few of us really understand. This is what the Oxford Dictionary says:

> *Fraud: 1. Criminal deception; the use of false representations*
>
> *to gain an unjust advantage. 2. A dishonest artifice or trick.*
>
> *3. A person or thing not fulfilling what is claimed or expected*
>
> *of it.*

Were you deceived by false representations? Did anyone in the chain of events leading up to your acquisition gain an unjust advantage (like taking money from you)? Did you believe you were acquiring a legitimate product? Did it fulfil what was expected?

You may think the mere idea of boiler room scams existing in 2022 is far-fetched and that it belongs only in movies like The Sting, which is set in 1936. However, in 2018 five people were jailed for a total of nearly 18 years for their involvement in a complex London-based boiler room scam that resulted in £2.8m losses.

The Financial Conduct Authority brought the criminal prosecution after carrying out a probe into five different boiler room companies, one of which claimed to be "one of the UK's largest wealth advisory firms". The FCA alleged that between July 2010 and April 2014 members of the public were persuaded to invest in a company that owned land on the island of Madeira. Investors were told the land — and therefore the company's shares — would increase in value to give returns of as much as 228%, but none were ever paid. More than 170 investors lost money in the scam. The court found the defendants guilty of offences of conspiracy to defraud, fraud, money laundering and perverting the course of justice, as well as breaches of markets legislation. During "Operation Tidworth", as the case was dubbed, prosecutors found that defendants had forged documents under the name of the Four Seasons and Hilton Hotels as part of conning investors into thinking the hotel chains were interested in buying the Madeira development, for example.

The trial judge, His Honour Judge Hehir, said that "some victims have lost everything they had", adding that "those who commit these offences cannot expect anything but firm punishment".

The issue of knowledge requires further unpacking. To highlight this, we need to go back to The Twins introduction of their friends at RW Invest.

When the FCA wrote to us regarding the Royal Kings Arms Hotel we immediately told The Twins and RW Invest about the letter. We also made the FCA fully aware of the involvement of both entities. It is impossible to imagine a scenario where the FCA failed to contact both. In any event, we had various discussions with both about the matter and therefore can say without doubt that they were fully aware of the FCA`s concerns.

We could however be generous, give them the benefit of the doubt and accept that maybe they forgot about those encounters. But there`s another problem faced by RW Invest, one which digs their hole a lot deeper.

In May of 2021 UCIS Advice Point received a letter from Brandsmiths Solicitors acting on behalf of RW Invest. It followed letters being sent out by UAP to those investors who had purchased a unit in Reliance House, Liverpool informing them that the development appeared to be a UCIS, to which a number had responded. The development had been created by Legacie Developments which was not registered with or regulated by the FCA. We`ll return to Legacie Developments.

Brandsmiths letter to UAP accused the firm of a number of various counts of defamation and malicious falsehood and stated that "RW Invest take significant steps to ensure that all of its investments are regulated." Over seven pages their letter set out their claims which included:

"Your letters contain a number of false statements and is a direct, unmerited and malicious attacks on our client's reputation. For example, the Letters state that:

a.   "we are aware that you have invested into the above-mentioned scheme";

b. "Many developers of these types of schemes have gone into administration;"

c. "you may have acquired the property in an unlawful Unregulated Collective Investment Scheme";

d. "likely to be unlawful";

e. "you may have been wrongly advised to purchase in this particular scheme";

f. "can NOT be marketed to the general public";

g. "it appears that you have invested into an unlawful development"; and

h. "your investment within what appears to be an Unregulated Collective Investment Scheme".

Your publication of the Statements together, and each of them, amounts to defamation of our clients pursuant to the Defamation Act 2013, and/or malicious falsehood."

They ended by requesting a swift apology to their client, payment of "yet to be agreed damages" and three thousand pounds towards their legal costs. UAP duly responded refuting all allegations and pointing out the various errors and assumptions made whilst ensuring they were fully conversant with the relevant law. Ultimately, no further accusations or proceedings were raised by RW Invest or their solicitors.

Let`s now return to Legacie Developments. The RW Invest website merely describes the developer as Legacie Developments. Companies House has two entities with that name, almost. Legacie Developments Limited was incorporated on the 13th of August 2018. Currently, it has one single director, John Morley. Legacie Developments Ordsall Lane Ltd was incorporated on the 10th of July 2020. Mr Morley is also a director of this company. Other directors include, Michael Gledhill, the current director of RW Invest Manchester Ltd, RW Invest London Ltd and RW Invest Holdings Ltd. Julian Ramsden resigned his directorship on the 20th of January 2022 along with, it seems, just about every other directorship he had including a number in companies bearing the name "Nexus Residential" a name which corresponds with other developments in this arena. The only current directorship maintained by Mr Ramsden (as at the point of publication) is in JR Invest LLP and JR Invest Holdings Ltd.

It seems clear from the information held at Companies House that RW Invest and Legacie Developments are intrinsically linked. In fairness to them, they are not the first or only organisation to recognise the benefits of an effective sales team and morphing into a developer. Jerald Solis did the same when his Experience Invest sales company closed down. A notice dated 31st December 2020 on experienceinvest.co.uk now says,

We hope you and your family are all well at this current time. The past year has presented significant challenges for Experience Invest and after 16 years of trading, it is with great sadness that we are now faced with a position where we have no alternative but to close the company and cease trading. From today, we will no longer be available to assist in any ongoing operations relating to your property investment and moving forwards you will need to contact your relevant management company or investor group directly. We would like to take this opportunity to wish you the very best for the future along with your current and future property investments.

Best regards,
Experience Invest

This is not of course, the end of Mr Solis as he has morphed into a developer of, amongst other things student accommodation with a sizeable brand offering what appear to be unregulated collective investment schemes, at least one of which has suffered issues with various planning issues and UAP have already been contacted by some investors.

If you can sell, why wouldn't you sell for yourself. After all, there doesn't appear to be a law against that – unless you're selling unregulated collective investment schemes.

Our Hit List doesn`t only have 450 individual developments on it but details of all the sales agents who have been selling these unlawful schemes. If you want to check out any agent, just drop me an email.

CHAPTER 5

What Do You Call 500 Lawyers At The Bottom of The Sea?

A start! Make crime pay, become a lawyer! Lawyers are men who will swear black is white - if they are paid for it! How many lawyer jokes are there? One, the rest are all true stories!

Enough already. If you're thinking that I might just have something of a complex where lawyers are concerned, you may well be right.

I've spent most of my life surrounded by lawyers and one or two I even call friends. But my experience of working with them and for them is anything but encouraging. As an employee I found them spineless. As a contractor undertaking work for them, they have often been underhand and dishonest. I have lost hundreds` of thousands of pounds to their duplicity, and, as someone described it, slipperiness. One, who is currently managing a significant claim for an equally significant law firm was even described to me by a fellow member of his profession as "a practising charlatan!" But then, I imagine that most professions have a small percentage of bad apples.

It's more than forty years since I first walked into the office of a local solicitor's firm as an employee. I'd like to say I'm not sure why but I can't.

At about twelve years of age, I declared to my parents that I wanted to be a lawyer. I have absolutely no idea why I said that as there was nothing in my family background to lead me to it. As a result, my father arranged for me to meet "the family solicitor". It sounded grand back then I suppose, but we didn't own any great estates, merely a three-bed semi in Stoke-on-Trent. I remember the meeting but absolutely nothing about it apart from feeling a bit like a royal child being introduced to his future principal. And therein lies a clue to the problem of lawyers.

Arrogance.

The legal profession breeds arrogance like maggots breed flies. Ask any fisherman who has ever forgotten to empty a bait box after a session on the river and they'll tell you that all those juicy little morsels that fish go cock-a-hoop for have now turned into thousands of flies. Dead flies.

I had enough arrogance of my own back then, but I remember very clearly the thoughts I had as I walked to the local court. The Magistrates and County Courts were built above a two-storey car park and there were four or five flights of external concrete steps to get to the top. I used to count each one and on hitting the summit remind myself that I was on top of the world, above everything and everybody. I carried that unrecognised baggage for a long time. Until, in fact, life threw me a curve ball and knocked the chip off my shoulder.

Sadly, I've seen that arrogance in far too many lawyers I've encountered. Even some I've known from the very early days of my legal career and went to law college with. The level of arrogance they display is monumental and they believe they are above everything. I suspect this is to do with the often-misplaced belief that they know the law and have been given the knowledge and tools to argue their way out of any given situation. They come to believe that they are Teflon-coated. I've seen how in some cases it has affected the firms they worked in and ran as their behaviour ultimately caused the downfall of the firm and bought their disgrace when struck off the roll of practicing solicitors.

A few years ago, a lawyer sat down at a meeting in my office in Blackpool. He was middle-aged, a partner in the law firm he was representing and accompanied by a junior female solicitor. He was meeting to discuss acting for all the purchasers of room investments in a hotel development. His firm had been introduced by sales agents – a familiar pattern of behaviour that we'll return to. There was concern from the potential developer, that what was being offered might amount to a UCIS. The lawyer had driven from Yorkshire for the meeting and commented openly to the client that during the drive to Blackpool he had come to the conclusion that he wasn't "bothered if you're running an unregulated collective investment scheme because you're going to jail, not me!".

Abdication is generally associated only with sitting monarchs. The Oxford English Dictionary defines "abdicate" as to "renounce one's duty or responsibility. It is safe to say that the lawyers acting in all cases of UCIS have abdicated. Completely. Some have done so on the way in, and again on the way out.

One name that crops up frequently when looking at these schemes is that of TQ Property Lawyers. If you look at some of the schemes and individuals TQ have been involved with it comes as no great surprise to see them popping up everywhere.

TQ Property Lawyers Limited was incorporated on 8th February 2012 by Iain Robert Tenquist and Gareth Rhys Jones. At the time, the occupation of each man was stated as Licensed Conveyancer. However, it appears that Mr Tenquist was admitted as a solicitor on the $1^{st \, of}$ February 1984 while Mr Jones was admitted as a solicitor on 5th January 2009. You might wonder why anyone chooses to downgrade their professional credentials. TQ also appeared to have some sort of fetish for large boards of directors and looking at their current website it looks like they appointed anyone and everyone who worked at the firm apart from the office dog – all good offices have an office dog these days. From the information held at Companies House TQ Property Lawyers Ltd had no fewer than ten directors. Yes, ten (10). Now, I've been to their office in Leigh, Lancashire and it resembled a two-bedroomed terraced house and certainly wasn't the offices of a major corporate entity. A quick check at Companies House tells me that the international plant and machinery manufacturer JCB, whose factory is the size of about ten football pitches and employs more than six thousand staff in the UK alone has only six directors. One of the largest privately-owned restaurant groups in the UK is Gordon Ramsey Restaurants and they have two directors. Even Lord Sugar only has eight directors in his property empire holding company, Amshold International Ltd.

No doubt Tenquist and Jones had their reasons but whatever they were a Winding Up order was issued against TQ Property Lawyers Ltd on the 21$^{st\,of}$ October 2020. It followed a flurry of directorship resignations earlier in June 2020 when it would seem the brown stuff started to hit the fan.

It's possible that the fan was started by problems at Mederco, the developer of a number of developments that subsequently failed. Student Developments. We know for instance, that TQ acted for at least one investor (and therefore quite probably many more) who had acquired a unit in Cardiff Student Village for sixty-five thousand pounds in July 2018 and that Mederco was falling apart at the seams by April 2019. It would be likely that claims for losses would start to hit the relevant lawyers within a year.

Fortunately, Tenquist had another company up his sleeve. Formerly known as Tenquists Limited and then Tenquists Solicitors Limited, TQ Law Limited had been incorporated on the 11$^{th\,of}$ June 2012. According to the SRA it has been a recognised body, authorised for all legal services since

78

November 2012 and this would mean that the principals would not need to seek authorisation for a new firm when the first was liquidated. This company operates from the same address in Leigh as its predecessor. It is also regulated by the Solicitors Regulation Authority and accredited by the Law Society for its "Conveyancing Quality", and one must therefore assume nothing but good about this new firm. Certainly, Mr Tenquist appears to be enjoying himself on one of the website photographs where he is portrayed with a bevy of young ladies, a dozen or more all looking like they're set for a night out while their boss seems to have his sleeves rolled up in readiness for something.

Mr Tenquist is the Chairman of the new firm and appears to be joined by at least six others on the board. But sadly, still no dog.

It's clearly obvious that Iain Robert Tenquist isn't the only lawyer to have been involved in the conveyancing of unregulated collective investment schemes. There are a lot more. However, before moving on to others it's important to stick with TQ for a little longer as the story only gets more interesting.

You'll remember, from the beginning of this story mention of The Twins, the two guys who provided everything needed for the hotel project in Lancaster. You'll remember also that they introduced Julian Ramsden at RW Invest. I can now reveal that Ramsden introduced none other than TQ Property Lawyers to act on behalf of all the investors who would ultimately buy the rooms. TQ acted on the majority of forty-three room sales.

When the letter from the FCA landed in late 2014, telling us that they considered the Lancaster scheme to be a UCIS one of the first things we did was to inform all those concerned. Together with Ross Wellman I went to meet directly with Iain Tenquist at his office in Leigh, near Wigan in Lancashire. We set out the FCA's argument clearly and told him that the project needed to be properly restructured to the satisfaction of the FCA and that we had employed Mischon de Reya to undertake that process.

Initially, Tenquist was very understanding and supportive of what we were trying to do, and Ross Wellman and I came away from the meeting reasonably content. Tenquist then did an about turn, changing his mind and claiming that the project was not a UCIS. If the FCA think it is, then it is, we told him. Sadly, he then informed all investors in the project that it wasn't a UCIS and didn't need restructuring and made everyone's role in that unnecessarily harder.

The real point to be made here is about knowledge. It was December 2014 when the FCA intervened in the Lancaster project and when they were made aware of all the people involved. We also know that the SRA were involved and spoke with Setfords and Ross Wellman. If they spoke with Ross about his handling of the sales, they almost certainly will have spoken to TQ about theirs.

It's difficult to believe anything other than Ian Tenquist has known about the issue of unregulated collective investment schemes since 2015. In fact, together with Ross Wellman, I personally made him aware of this in January 2015. And yet in 2018 he was acting for purchasers in the Cardiff Student Village project being developed by Stuart Day at Mederco and which subsequently went into administration. I was also introduced to Mr Day by Matthew Longworth (who you'll come across again later) as we sat outside the very fashionable Scott's of Mayfair in London.

But what is perhaps even more startling is that Tenquists' regulatory body, The Solicitors Regulating Authority (SRA) have been openly warning all solicitors to avoid these types of schemes since at least 2014, and possibly earlier. The following are extracts from their updated "Warning Notice" for lawyers:

> *This warning notice is relevant to solicitors and all law firms, their managers and employees.*
>
> *We have warned for a number of years about the risks posed by dubious or questionable investment schemes.*
>
> ***Our expectations***
>
> *We expect you to act with integrity and protect consumers by robustly analysing the risks of any investment scheme you are involved in. The obligation rests on you as a firm to carry out all necessary checks and you should not rely on the word of the seller or other promoters of a scheme.*

Our concerns

We continue to receive reports about law firms that are involved in dubious or questionable investment schemes. We are seeing:

Solicitors and law firms being used to give credibility to a scheme rather than because legal work is required. These sorts of schemes have been highlighted in previous warnings issued by us

Dubious or risky schemes being presented as routine conveyancing or investment in "land" when the reality is very different

Conveyancing or purported investment in land

Buyer-led financing of a development

Schemes are being promoted as involved in the routine buying of a property when in reality the buyer's money is being used to finance a high-risk development or refurbishment. This is of particular concern in unusual developments such as the buying of individual hotel rooms, rooms in care homes, or self-storage units.

Taking a lease of a room, a storage unit etc

Schemes are being promoted by which buyers take a lease of a supposed asset such as a hotel room, care home room, parking space or self- storage unit. This list is not exhaustive as fraudsters will continue to search for similar 'assets'.

These 'fractional property' investments are where the buyer buys a portion or fraction of an investment property and receives a fraction of the rental income....They were typically marketed as being 'a low-cost, high-yield investment product that's hands off and hassle free'.

Collective investment schemes – criminal liability

Many of these schemes are likely to be 'collective investment schemes' under section 235 of the Financial Services and Markets Act 2000. Collective investment schemes are defined in the FCA Handbook Glossary (see link). If those involved in the schemes are not authorised by FCA, they will be committing a criminal offence and are likely to be imprisoned. You should exercise caution when being invited to be involved in any scheme that appears to involve a collective investment element.

Our view is that buyer-led schemes are likely to be regarded as collective investment schemes because the buyers are required to pool their money together, for example to finance the construction of a building.

Conclusion

You must not facilitate or arrange dubious or fraudulent investments. For all investments or products that are regulated by the FCA, you must make sure that you are permitted to do so. In addition, you must rigorously assess the transaction and refuse or cease to act if there is any doubt about the propriety of the transaction or whether buyers are being misled in any way. If you fail to make proper enquiries you could find yourself in breach of some or all of our Principles and standards. You could also be found to have acted dishonestly.

Red flags

Be alert to these sorts of issues:

- *comparatively high returns*
- *guaranteed buy-back of a product or property for profit*
- *sellers ask firms to promote the scheme or appear in marketing material*
- *buyers are mainly from another jurisdiction to the location of the scheme*
- *high commissions due to sellers from deposits*

(The above list was extracted from a list of 12 "Red Flags)

You can be forgiven for wondering just how Iain Robert Tenquist will explain why he has avoided the advice of his regulator for so long. Having already stated why these investments are considered "dubious" and as the schemes as "fraudulent" the SRA conclude with "You must not facilitate" them.

With something like four hundred and fifty UCIS schemes out there (that we currently know about) it`s clear that Iain Tenquist was not the only lawyer undertaking this, to quote the SRA "dubious" type of work.

CHAPTER 6

The Good, The Bad, and The Thoroughly Misled

Over the last few years and through the work done by UCIS
Advice Point I have come into contact with lots of investors. As
many as two thousand or more individuals have approached
UAP because they have lost money on failed UCIS schemes.
The vast majority were very nice people who had only wanted a
secure retirement but ended up with a millstone around their
neck and needed help to be freed of it.

There are some who I have become really quite friendly
with, in a remote, virtual manner, but who I'd happily take out
to dinner. However, there is something of a misconception
about this group of people. They were not all seriously wealthy
or sophisticated investors. They do however, all share a single
identifying characteristic, one which I sincerely hope will not
upset those I refer to as friends. They were naïve. And some
were blatantly stupid.

The type of individual investor is also interesting. There are
doctors, IT specialists, retired bankers, Middle Eastern
businessmen, and even finance directors who really should have
known better. I even recall a successful businessman based on

one of the more exotic Caribbean islands buying four hotel rooms. And then there`s Mrs Jones, who is looking to invest the insurance policy monies received after her husband has died.

What each and every one sought was simple. Security and income.

Why were they naïve or stupid? Firstly, they forgot the age-old maxim: If it looks too good to be true it probably is! Secondly, who pays out five thousand pounds as a deposit on something they`ve never actually seen and gives it to someone they`ve never actually met. And to that five grand you can probably add another one as all sales agencies, certainly at the time of these sales, also asked for a fee of one thousand or more to do business with them.

One particular investor paid deposits on five units but then couldn`t get answers to certain queries and just walked away without getting his deposits back. You will be forgiven for thinking that he had more money than sense!

The unfortunate reality of this is that every one of the investors in these failed schemes was taken in by a smooth-talking salesman.

Danny Law is a London based investor who purchased a room in a Pinnacle Student development in Liverpool known as The Paramount. In 2016 he paid £55,000 and was told he would receive an annual return on his investment of 9% for five years. He received less than the "guaranteed" figure for the first year, after which payments ceased. Pinnacle were also responsible for failed developments known as Quadrant, also in Liverpool, and Spectrum in Sheffield.

Danny Law said, "This affects so many people who have lost their life savings that were set aside for retirement or their grandchildren`s university fees and no-one is doing anything to stop it." He also has a further investment in the A1 Alpha failed scheme at Park Lane, Sunderland.

However, the Pinnacle developments are merely the tip of an iceberg. According to research we carried out at UAP there are at least two hundred and fifty individual developments of this kind in the UK. The number is growing as unscrupulous developers continue to market these schemes.

When approached about Pinnacle and another development The FCA said, "Offering investments in property is not regulated by the FCA. However, some property investments can be structured as collective investment schemes if the investment is in the scheme rather than in the underlying property. This requires, amongst other things, that the operating firm is authorised by the FCA and complies with certain minimum disclosure obligations. It is a criminal offence to operate a collective investment scheme without FCA authorisation. "Collective investment schemes are considered high risk and are aimed at sophisticated and high net worth investors. Consumers investing in them should be prepared to lose all their money. We recommend investors check the FCA Register to find out whether a collective investment scheme is regulated by the FCA. We are unable to comment specifically on Daniel Johns or Pinnacle Student Developments other than to say that it was not authorised by the FCA."

Similarly, Ray and his wife are retired. He is in his mid-seventies but still in good health. In around 2017 they invested one hundred and twenty thousand pounds for two rooms in a student accommodation block in Bradford known as Scholars Village. They were promised returns of 10% per annum which never materialised. The development was one of about twenty others undertaken by Derek Kewley and Nicholas Spence using a variety of newly incorporated shell companies.

Together with UCIS Advice Point I worked closely with Ray and finally managed to initiate a scheme to recover their losses, now being run by solicitors and moving towards a likely settlement with insurers. There are around two hundred and fifty claims in that scheme.

When Ray and his wife invested part of their retirement funds into the Scholars Village scheme, they thought they were buying into an investment that would provide them with an attractive income for the rest of their lives. Nothing could have been further from the truth.

With promised returns ranging from 8% to 10% over ten years they handed over their hard-earned cash to purchase two student accommodation 'units'.

Ray says: 'It looked perfect for us. We were living in France at the time, so we didn't want an investment that we had to manage ourselves like a buy-to-let property. We were investing into property which everyone thinks of as secure, and our solicitors didn't warn of any reason why we shouldn't proceed.' Ray thought it would be an 'armchair investment' - one where he and Lois could sit back and pocket the income from the rent paid by the students.

Within eighteen months, the promised fixed annual returns on their investment had dried up. The company that managed all the properties, A1 Alpha Properties (Leicester) Limited went into administration with directors Kewley and Spence partly blaming its collapse on a glut of student accommodation. Investors collectively stand to lose up to £100 million as a result of the business failure - and to rub salt into open wounds they continued to receive demands for service charges and ground rents. And whilst the management company may have gone into liquidation the same cannot be said of the development companies used by Kewley and Spence, at least some of which remain active with the same two directors.

Despite the warnings from the FCA these types of schemes continue to be offered to unwary buyers. Agents are still offering high level returns of 8 to 10% per annum for these so-called investments. The Baltic Hotel and Epic hotel in Liverpool along with the Comfort Inn Manchester are all examples of this type of risky investment. Many of the "agents" will be developers marketing their own projects.

When approached for his thoughts Gareth Shaw, Head of Money, Which?, said: "High-risk schemes that lure investors with the promise of high returns have become increasingly prevalent, but as they are unregulated and do not offer the same protections as traditional schemes savers should be aware that they could lose everything if something goes wrong. The regulator must keep a closer eye on these types of schemes to ensure they are transparent with investors about the risks involved. Savers looking to invest must also be wary of high-risk investments. Use the FCA's database to check if a company is regulated and remember - if it seems too good to be true then it probably is."

If some people are fortunate to escape these scams suffering only the financial loss others are not quite so fortunate. I received the following (unedited) email from Dirk on May 31st, 2022:

Hi Neil,

So here is my story.

A brief history. Born 1956.

Left school with no qualifications and completed my time as a plumber's apprentice.

Married at 19, purchased 1st house aged 20 so doing ok.

Fast forward to 2006, we moved to Spain and established a successful property rental and pool maintenance business from scratch. 2013 I transferred my private pension to a company based in Spain as informed it was more tax efficient with better annual rates. Within 12 months I had issues with the company.

2016 we decided to take early retirement and move back to UK to enjoy our new grandchildren and look after our aging parents. We sold the business and moved back in July 2016.

The following September I was made aware purely by chance that the pension company had folded. This is a long complicated saga but basically I lost 80% of my pension. As we retired early we knew and planned to live quite frugal until eligible for our state pension so to lose this was a big hit.

So 2017 we decided with our remaining savings to make what we thought was a safe investment in a Hotel which would supplement the losses on pension and our income. The fact it was advertised on Rightmove via a leading award winning estate agent in Cheshire gave us confidence in this. (It seems this agent was a front for another agent with a chequered history)

Also that the solicitors were a large established company AND obtaining land registry titles gave us 100% peace of mind with the purchase. At no time did we receive what we would class as a clear concise warning of this type of investment being high risk.

The Hotel is a Grade 2 listed property in a fabulous position in a very popular resort so all seemed great. The investment promised 10% p.a. returns with 125% buyback after 10 years plus an added bonus of 2 weeks B&B annual usage, very handy as living on a tight budget. Cost was £75k.

Another supporting factor was that another project of NPD was the Afan Valley resort supported by Ken Skates of Welsh Government, Sir Peter Moore, formally of Centre Parcs but now with NPD and Bear Grylls gave this company strong creditability.

We knew when we viewed the Hotel that it required upgrading and NPD made this clear with big plans in very high quality brochures and website.

During the first year of visits it became very concerning that very few improvements had been done and the cleanliness and maintenance was very poor. I had reason to complain strongly to management and NPD head office. The following year nothing improved.

Our first payment of £7500 was due February 2019, I spoke to head office and was informed there was a two week delay. Nothing received so I had a lengthy conversation with Gavin Woodhouse who assured me everything was ok and a new accounting and computer structure was being implemented. I received a letter from him informing me that a pro rata payment would be made in July of £10200.

6 days before the payment was due the leading story on ITV news was about the collapse and fraud investigation into NPD, hence we never received any payments. So to date we are missing 4 payments totalling £30k

To say we were gutted is an understatement, scammed twice in 3 years was beyond belief as have always been cautious with money.

A few weeks after this I had a minor breakdown.

My confidence has been affected, I suffer anxiety, have considered suicide several times and feel embarrassed and angry more than ever. Fortunately we have a strong marriage and very close supportive family. This affected our daily lives due to the constant lack of money even for the simple things in life. We have never been out of work, sometimes having two jobs and never had any benefits from the state system. Embarrassingly we have been having to live on £860 p.m. Universal credit for the last two years. If we take my 91 year old mother for a meal, which isn't as often as should be she pays as we have no spare money

Most annoying is the fact this could have been future money for our grandchildren but instead supports the parasite Gavin Woodhouse to have his Grade 1 mansion, Rolex collection and fleet of luxury cars and expensive holidays.

We often say things could be a lot worse and they could but this doesn't make it easier.

Fortunately we will both be eligible for our state pension July so at least can have some normality again.

We can now just hope the Hotel sells soon and we get something back but won't be much going by the sales in

Llandudno. A huge wish is to see Gavin Woodhouse, his wife and his comrades in court, given hefty sentences and all assets seized but knowing the weak UK system this won't happen. He is already being allowed privileged and confidential investigation, with several court dates postponed, unbelievable.

Unfortunately this is crime without violence, nobody physically hurt, no blood, visible wounds, weapons etc so nobody sees the damage to the victims but £80m scammed.

If this was a £1m bank robbery with guns it would be a huge investigation.

I have done a few media interviews but today's news is tomorrow's history.

Hope this doesn't waffle too much.

Regards

D

The historic Hever Castle is located close to the village of Edenbridge in Kent, some 30 miles south-east of London. It was built in the 13th century and from 1462 to 1539, it was the home of the family of Anne Boleyn the second queen of King Henry the 8th and is now open to the public as a tourist attraction. It`s also the site of Hever House Hotel which may not be as historic but is equally notorious.

Whether that was the reasoning behind Brentwood based John Francis's purchase of a room in the hotel's sister property, Needham House back in 2013/14 I'm not sure. But with a price tag of £200K it seems reasonable to think that this investor saw something of interest.

As usual, he was promised a guaranteed return of 10% for 10 years, with the developer agreeing to buy back rooms after five years at the original purchase price.

The developer at Needham House, Oak Property Partners Ltd, raked in £15.7million. Incorporated by director Darren Popely in 2012, it is now in liquidation. Similarly, in a scenario which is all too familiar the developer at Hever was sister company Oak Forest Partnership Limited, which took about £10million and is also in liquidation. Its directors were Popely, Paul Gould, who has since died, and Stephen Dickson. The hotels operator White Linen Hotel and Resorts Ltd, directed by Popely and Gould, is in liquidation too.

Wind back about thirteen years and it seems that the Hever Castle site was the venue for a failed timeshare operation run by businessman and horse breeder, Ronald Popely, father of Darren Popely. Investors poured £7 million into his scheme before it collapsed. Popely was subsequently banned from being a director of any company until 2012.

In an interesting twist some buyers in these schemes bought their rooms with mortgages from off-shore company Mercantile Investment Holdings SA, which was part-owned by Stephen

Dickson. They received "mortgages" of half the purchase price from the hotels' owner, which is the parent of the company running the investment scheme. It then proceeded to repossess rooms from investors who had failed to keep up with mortgage payments. These were supposed to be taken out of the room rental payments due to investors, but these "guaranteed" amounts were not being paid as the hotel was not as profitable as the forecast provided at the point of sale.

Purchasers of the rooms were recommended to use solicitors Graham & Rosen of Hull, but its "Head of Investment Property" Sheena Taylor was not even a qualified solicitor and has since been banned from working for law firms for "manifest incompetence" in yet another property investment scheme.

Rose and Peter Edkins, both in their late 60s, purchased a room at the Hever Hotel to help to fund their retirement. The couple said they had entered a "foul nightmare" following the collapse of the scheme. "We have been stripped of rental income of £1,500 per month which was the core of our retirement funding, and very likely of our £180,000 investment," Mrs Edkins said.

The Hever and Needham affairs have also had a lasting effect on investors, and some have lost everything. At least one lost an inheritance, while another was made homeless as a result of her financial difficulties. Another said, "This was supposed to be our pension, but the whole scheme feels like it was made up."

In June 2022 the Insolvency Service announced that the company's liquidation had triggered an investigation which revealed that the directors made £20.6 million worth of payments, including £7.1 million paid to connected companies. Ronald Popely also acted as a director of the company, including for two years which were in direct breach of his previous 9-year ban.

The Secretary of State for Business, Energy and Industrial Strategy accepted disqualification undertakings from all three directors, which prevents them from directly, or indirectly, becoming involved in the promotion, formation or management of a company, without the permission of the court.

Stephen Dickson was the first director to be banned and his 7-year disqualification commenced on 29 April 2022. Both Ronald and Darren Popely received 9-year bans, which began on 12 May and 18 May respectively.

The room owners at the two hotels are currently engaged with insolvency experts Grant Thornton in a legal action to recover the hotels and go on to manage the properties to enable investors to recover some of their losses.

Hong Kong-based Kevin Leung paid £62,000 for a unit in Daniel Johns' Regent 88 office block in Liverpool and which doesn't appear to even exist. He says: 'Despite my room being registered at the Land Registry it still hasn't been formed and cannot be identified.'

All is not what it seems with Daniel Johns, or its alter ego D.J Suites. Daniel Johns is really Khalid Iqbal BHATTI, is a 38-year-old Pakistani man who claims to be a graduate of the University of Westminster, London. He allegedly changed his name to Daniel John to reflect a more international image in the company's promotional video, but his company website has since deleted his information. The company boasts a collective experience of 15 years, and says it operates across 7 countries worldwide.

According to its LinkedIn profile The Daniel Johns Group is the UK's most innovative real estate group with a combined experience of over 100 years – you'll note the subtle difference from the company's website which quotes 15 years. It goes on to say, "We are made up of six autonomous brands which further have a collection of highly successful real estate brands under their umbrellas. Our brands are unique, innovative yet very secure for real estate investors."

Unfortunately, DJ's clients appear not to agree with those statements and reviews on 192.com are 100% "Bad"!

Many of DJ's properties have been sold in China and the Far East. In October 2020 Apple Daily in Hong Kong found that DJ had as many as 21 development projects, including hotels, offices, and high-end serviced residences, spread over many major cities in the UK, such as London, Manchester, Liverpool and Blackpool. They said the company specialises in buying old properties, refurbishing and reselling them, to attract new investors into the market. After the group targeted the Hong Kong market in 2017, six projects went viral. It used intermediary companies to hold a number of trade fairs in Hong Kong, offering an annual rental return of 7% to 8%, and guaranteed to buy back the properties with an additional 10% to 30% above the original price after seven years. Due to the low investment threshold, many unwary investors from Hong Kong have poured their hard-earned money into the projects.

However, DJ`s hotel projects, THE ELEMENT, Blackpool, and London's REGENT 88 office project have been liquidated due to financial difficulties and the list includes the construction companies for serviced residential apartment 'One Boulevard' and Manchester HILUX. Meanwhile, the 1 KENSINGTON hotel project was burned down and turned into ruins. Many investors were caught by surprise and lost their investments.

DJ's sales office in Hong Kong has since closed down. DJ responded that there were problems with many projects. Among them, the management company responsible for THE ELEMENT, Blackpool, and REGENT 88 was liquidated due to financial problems.

Another one of DJ`s disasters was once Hull's first AA four-star hotel. Today the derelict former Portland Hotel casts a long shadow over the city and its fate is bound up in a tangled web of companies and on-going legal action.

Khalid Bhatti`s vision of creating resorts featuring luxury apartments, designer shopping malls and beauty spas contrasts sharply with the current state of the empty six-storey building in Hull. Recently, safety barriers were installed on the street to protect passers-by from falling masonry. Above an empty ground floor cafe which forms part of the building, several large wall tiles are no longer in place. Chunks of concrete which form some of the old hotel's upper floor window ledges also appear to be missing.

According to one nearby shop owner, there is also significant water damage inside the property as a result of holes in the roof - having seen them for herself last year. The businesswoman, who did not wish to be named, explained: "There was water coming through into my shop which is underneath the rear part of what used to be the hotel.

"At the time, there were some builders working on it and they took me up right up to the top floor and the roof. I couldn't believe what I saw. There were big holes in the roof. "They were only covered with black plastic bags to keep the rain out. The builders told me there is a lot of water damage inside. and I saw a lot of it myself."

The empty hotel property was acquired in 2013 for £600,000 by Grif Student Grounds Rents Ltd, a company which is part of the Ground Rents Income Fund, a real estate investment trust whose 19,000-strong portfolio of properties includes the Freedom Quay apartment block next to Hull Marina.

A month earlier, planning permission was secured to convert the hotel into student accommodation with 126 beds by a company called Crown Place Hull Ltd. Companies House records show Rafik Patel was the sole director and shareholder of Crown Place but by June 2016 the company had been dissolved. It's believed the property was briefly used to house students with ensuite rooms being advertised from £99 to £135 per week on 48-week leases before Crown Place was dissolved. Then, in August 2018, Grif Student Ground Rents Ltd. granted a 999-year lease on the property to Daniel Johns Hull Ltd. in a £400,000 deal.

It was at this stage that Mr Bhatti entered the story as the director of Daniel Johns Hull Ltd, one of several of his companies operating as part of his Daniel Johns Group (DJG) which he founded and chairs.

Accounts filed to Companies House show at various points the company's name has been changed six times while Mr Bhatti himself is currently listed as having held 57 different directorships. Some are still active but most of them are associated with either dissolved or liquidated companies. Mr Bhatti is also currently the sole director of DJ Suites Hull Ltd, which holds an under-lease at the property from DJG.

Shortly before leasing the Hull property, Mr Bhatti was busy elsewhere in Pakistan's capital Islamabad, launching his vision of luxury real estate investment in two cities in the country at a glitzy ceremony which is still featured in a YouTube video. Flanked by an array of models, celebrities and TV stars he set out his plans to build a complex aimed at attracting overseas investors who would be able to use their apartments for holiday breaks and then be rented out for the rest of the year.

He told his audience: "We don't just build properties, we build futures."

Official Land Registry documents show legal action has been taken and successfully resulted in vesting orders being granted in relation to 33 named investors, mostly believed to be from Hong Kong. The orders protect under-leases on rooms in their names within the empty hotel building.

Together with UCIS Advice Point I've worked closely with Neil Stockdale, a partner and solicitor at top 100 UK law firm Hugh James, as his firm have reviewed a scheme where investors bought similar units in developments in London and Liverpool from the Daniel Jones Group.

In one case, a Hong Kong-based investor paid £62,000 for a unit in an office block in Liverpool which has yet to be built. He has yet to receive a single penny on what was billed as a guaranteed rental return.

Neil Stockdale says: "Our initial investigations lead us to believe that all these clients have been unlawfully sold a UCIS and that the lawyers who acted for them were negligent in a variety of ways."

However, the situation surrounding the former Portland Hotel in Hull is unclear.

"We have looked into the title documents regarding this matter, and it appears that the freehold owner has granted a long lease to Daniel Johns Hull Limited, who have subsequently granted an underlease to DJ Suites Hull Ltd. It is unclear whether individual rooms were marketed to investors by the developer as individual sub-leases, having not been registered at the Land Registry which we would expect to see in such a circumstance. However, there is a number of Unilateral Notices relating to vesting orders registered against the freehold title. The beneficiaries of these vesting orders appear to be Asian which might suggest that the development has been marketed in Hong Kong, Malaysia etc, as we have seen with similar Daniel Johns schemes, however we are unable to confirm as we do not have access to the vesting orders. A common situation where a vesting order is applied for is when a dissolved company had contracted to sell its assets, but the goods were not transferred despite being paid for."

According to the Hong Kong-based media outlet Dimsum Daily, the Daniel Johns Group's sales office there recently closed with Hong Kong's Estate Agents Authority currently investigating complaints by investors involving at least 20 stalled development projects in the UK.

In another case, a client purchased a student property in Lancashire from Daniel Johns Group and entered a rental guarantee contract with an associated company Silver Hopkins Asset Management Ltd. After one year of agreed rent payments, Silver Hopkins Asset Management Ltd went into liquidation and the payments stopped.

It is abundantly clear that the Daniel Johns Group is a parent of many different companies and has a pattern of liquidating them, taking money from investors, and claiming bankruptcy to only set up a new company and start the cycle again. They have however, been very good at gaining publicity. The following article is from:

Hospitality and Catering News – Oct 2018

Innovative property management company, Daniel Johns Group, has announced the launch of Rock Spice, a high-end fusion food restaurant opening in Manchester this month.

The restaurant will focus on Asian fusion dining, with chefs taking inspiration from traditional Pakistani, Indian and Bangladeshi cuisines combined with Western influences, while also infusing traditional rock spice into each dish which has been used in Asian cooking for generations.

Daniel Johns Group has invested £10 million into the launch of the new premium dining concept, with Rock Spice restaurants set to open in Liverpool, Blackpool and London by the end of the year, and at an additional two sites by spring 2019.

There are also further expansion plans on the horizon, with the company aiming to open 20 – 25 Rock Spice restaurants throughout the UK within the next three years and plans to take the concept to Pakistan already in the pipeline.

Daniel Johns Group recently diversified its offering to revolutionise food franchise investments and currently holds a portfolio of multiple global brands including The Counter Custom Burgers, and Nancy's Pizzeria which currently boasts 27 restaurants throughout North America.

Khalid Iqbal, Chairman at Daniel Johns Group, said: "The new restaurant and lounge offers a unique dining experience; bringing together the best elements of cooking from around the world, along with a family-friendly atmosphere, bar area where guests can relax with a drink, and lighting to create a fantastic ambiance.

"Manchester's dining scene is one of the most robust in the UK, so we're immensely proud that we're able to bring our new high-end dining concept to the city.

"Authentic Pakistani food is something we're extremely passionate about, so we're looking forward to bringing this offering to Manchester and the rest of the North West, and are excited to see what the future has in store for our newest restaurant brand."

Apart from working alongside UAP and Neil Stockdale (amongst others) I can add a little personal knowledge here because I live in Blackpool, home to one of DJ`s developments.

I became aware of this development before it was even commenced. It sits almost on the corner of one of the main thoroughfares out of Blackpool`s main town centre and isn`t in a salubrious area. I`d been given the details by a sales agent and as soon as he said "Hornby Road", I was immediately surprised. He had provided me with a rather impressive brochure which displayed the front of the property. I remember thinking, there`s nothing like this on Hornby Road.

When I reached the destination, I drove up and down the road two or three times but couldn`t find any properties that resembled the pictures in the brochure. Looking closer, I realised it was a computer generated image (CGI) and I only succeeded in identifying the actual property by the adjoining rooftops and alleyway leading down one side of the property.

Daniel Johns claimed to have invested millions into the properties they developed. In this instance the properties were three or four old and decrepit terraced houses which could have been bought for around £150K due to their condition. As I looked further at the site it was clear that the CGI could not be replicated. I also knew that get the number of bedrooms they intended to sell meant that they would most likely resemble rabbit hutches.

When it eventually opened it was nothing like the brochure promised. Frequently closed and with a host of bad reviews it struggled to survive a single season.

Reviews

Gen Coin 28 February 2020 22:08

Hundreds of investors in dozens of developments from Daniel Johns Group say they were defrauded. Bought properties that were never completed (One Boulevard Manchester, etc.), serviced apartments that were after all just poor hotels, and basically investors bought the properties because DJ sold them…

Anonymous Guest 23 February 2020 18:11

Scam and fraud. Do not use this company.

Daniel Johns Ltd, Victoria Knight Ltd, Silver Hopkins Asset Management and Red Admiral Vintage Ltd are a real estate property scam. They steal money from hard working people, promise guaranteed returns/high returns/rent on your investment, then liquidate and…

Guest Guest 03 February 2020 22:14

I lost all my life savings because Daniel Johns Group stole my money. Terrible customer service. Investment property sham, scam and fraud. I regret buying a property from Daniel Johns Group Ltd.

When Graham Firth saw an advert for an 8 per cent return on an investment in student digs, he thought he had found a great deal. More people were going to university than ever before, and he was told the Paramount development in Liverpool was not only finished but occupied. However, after the 54-year-old finance director invested £58,500, it emerged that the building was far from complete, and his money vanished.

Stefan is based in Shenzhen, China and purchased two apartments in Kings Dock Mill, Liverpool. According to our friends at RW Invest Kings Dock Mill is:

"An Iconic New Development with a Mixture of One, Two and Three-Bedroom Flats and Townhouses

Kings Dock Mill is located on Tabley Street, and the residence couldn't be in a better location. Under half a mile from Liverpool ONE shopping centre and a quick stroll away from the edgy vibe of the Baltic Triangle, Kings Dock Mill is right at the core of Liverpool's history and culture.

A High Standard Living Experience Is Anticipated

With an ultra-modern design that boasts solid wood flooring, top-of-the-range kitchens with mood lighting illuminating high-gloss surfaces, and sustainable technologies such as eco-electric heating and low voltage LED lights, this development boasts some impressive qualities. Residents can also use a 24/7 concierge service and gain access to a peaceful outdoor courtyard.

Investment Overview

- Prices From **£175,000**
- **7%** NET Rental Return
- Earn Minimum of **£12,250** NET Rental Income Return pa
- Adjacent to Liverpool Waterfront
- 15% Below Market Value
- Fully Fitted Modern Kitchens
- Furniture Pack Available
- Hands-Off Investment

We can see immediately that all the necessary hallmarks of a classic UCIS are present. This is not remotely surprising as investors have been contacting UAP for some time about this and other developments where North West Development Consortium Ltd, (NWDC) formerly known as YPG Group Ltd was involved. The company went into liquidation last year.

A report by the Insolvency Service states that NWDC owed £9,126,084.34 to creditors, many of whom are local independent companies, but this is unlikely to include any debt to investors. According to the same figures £3.8m is owed to YPG related companies. YPG is effectively Ming Yeung, and it seems that he has already gained more than a degree of notoriety. At least one investor called me and was clearly worried after a conversation with Yeung.

The website Property Tribes works hard to help investors caught up in scams, despite receiving more than their fair share of personal attacks from dodgy developers. These are just a few posts about Ming Yeung and YPG:

John 1 Apr 2021 at 19:29

I am posting the below which I posted on another forum.

This is becoming a bit concerning to me and I am worried about losing a lot of money. Does anyone have any further information please? After seeing what happened with Signature and Lawless - is this going to be another problem development? No reply to my emails and calls from YPG or RWI.

I just read that the while development has been sold to Nexus Residential on bdaily (please google it, can't post link). Directors of Nexus are also directors of RWI. How can the same properties be sold twice? I have been trying to call people all day without success.

Nexus and Legacie have worked on The Rise development in very similar circumstances to us. Kerry Tomlinson is even under investigation for that project by insolvency services: ("please google Kerry Tomlinson under investigation", can't post link). This is going to be my worst Easter........ Can any of you help please? You mentioned a group, can I please join?

Same here! Ming Yeung is playing games. Im an investor of KDM. Please count me in if there is a group of investors teaming up.

Hi,

I'm not an investor, but I was a previous tenant at Pembroke Studios by YPG and I've been struggling to recover my deposit of £650 for the last 6 months now.

I will most likely be taking this matter to court, but I was wondering if I could use any of this information to prove my point that Ming Yeung is a crook.
I'd also appreciate any advice etc.

Thank you
F

Hi Charlie,

Please drop me an email at kdminvestorgroup and I will explain where we are as a group. I'm not allowed to post the email address correctly, but it is a gmail address Thanks!

Yeung claims that although some of the YPG schemes were behind schedule, the liquidation of NWDC was not a particular concern. He suggested that the pandemic had caused major problems for his company but "This does not affect any of the projects as it was a construction company and didn't own any property.......Fabric Residence had its delays initially because funding for the scheme was hampered due to legal constraints. Under recent case law, a funder would normally get a first charge (a type of mortgage) and that would suffice. However, recently funding has been difficult due to unilateral notices (granted to buyers of apartments) placed upon the title by onward purchasers, which previously had no bearing on funders. We tried very hard to get funding and after a long period we finally found a lender that would assist despite the unilateral notices."

It has to be said that Yeung's claims raise lots of questions. Not least of all, why does he need funding when according to RW Invest, they are now selling the "Final Phase" in the development of 208 "fully managed" apartments being sold at a minimum price of £75,950. A quick Google search tells us that final phase means:

the end of something. type of: conclusion, ending, finish. event whose occurrence ends something.

That being the case it doesn't seem unreasonable to assume Yeung is now selling the final fifty or so apartments, meaning he's already raked in around £12 million. As for funding being "difficult due to unilateral notices (granted to buyers of apartments) placed upon the title" what did he expect.

One thing is certain, the investors caught up in these schemes didn't get what they expected. Whilst some are now in active claim groups and on their way to recovering at some of their losses many are still floundering and wondering what to do. Even as I write this I've had an investor on the telephone, following receipt of a letter from UAP who still doesn't understand what he should be doing and is more concerned with claims from a management company for the cost of new windows. It's an illegal scheme I told him. You should not be paying anything.

But if there's one issue that has caused many investors problems and delays in getting their money back it's probably the investors themselves. When the roof collapses on these schemes the investors understandably begin to come together in a common cause, for that's what it should be. Having found each other they then begin to form a group, generally on WhatsApp. It's always private and can rarely be penetrated.

The "pack" effect then kicks in as there's always more than one who thinks they should lead because they can shout louder. At first the group splinters into two and then possibly more. This of course means that there will now be more than one source of professional advice, and which brings its own problems, and the groups start to head off

in completely different directions. One wants to go after the developer, chasing monies around the world by way of a worldwide freezing order (and in doing so also doing the administrators job for them) and the others go off to court to recover in other ways.

The result is inevitable and is only likely to end in tears. As a lawyer said to me only a few days ago, about a group he is involved in, "it`s absolute carnage".

CHAPTER 7

Playground Monitors

Finding anyone with a good word to say about the FCA is like searching the proverbial haystack for that illusive needle. The regulator does not appear to have endeared itself to anyone, whether they are a regulated business or an investor. In fact, there are a great many investors who will say that the Financial Conduct Authority is failing in its duty to protect them. Moreover, to compensate them.

However, before we walk them to the gallows let's examine precisely what the role of this financial regulator really is.

The FCA was established on April 1st, 2013, and it took over from the Financial Services Authority (FSA). According to their website they exist to ensure markets work well for individuals, businesses, and the economy as a whole. They regulate the conduct of around 51,000 businesses and employ around 4,200 people. That sounds like quite a lot of staff bearing in mind that one of the constant complaints about the FCA is how slow they can be to respond. Ultimately, they`re looking for financial markets to be "fair and effective" so that consumers get a fair deal.

So, just how effective is the FCA? To answer this question, we`ll look firstly at a matter in which they don`t appear to have been as effective as many people think they should have been.

In December 2015 it was reported that Store First, the self-storage brand of UK based real estate developer Group First, had been accused of conducting a pension-fraud scheme, pocketing more than £100 million in investment through sales company Jackson Francis Ltd. Various marketing materials, including a video, reportedly made investment-return guarantees, which according to investors didn't materialise. Store First said it was unaware of the allegations and wasn't responsible for the sales strategies deployed by Jackson Francis.

On May 30th, 2022, Andrew emailed me from Dorset, England.

From: A
Sent: 30 May 2022 18:34

To: neil@neilbromage.com

Subject: Property Scams

Hello Neil,

You must, I am sure, be aware of the Park First "scam" involving the sale of leasehold car park spaces near Glasgow and Gatwick airports between 2015 and 2018.

Leases for about 12,000 car park spaces were sold all told, for prices that raised over £200 million from 4,500 investors in UK, Europe, and several countries in the Far East including Malaysia, Indonesia, Singapore, Taiwan and Hong Kong.

The sales material included RICS valuations for the car park spaces that – in hindsight – were ludicrously high, but which many buyers relied upon in their decision making.

The FCA became aware of the offering and told Park First that they were offering an unregulated collective investment and should desist from so doing.

I believe it is a story of interest to the public. I myself invested £250k on behalf of my wife and myself to increase our pension income, while I was working in Kuala Lumpur for Shell Malaysia on my last assignment before retirement.

I have been part of the Creditor's Committee during the Administration phase which has been managed by a large London firm of Insolvency Practitioners.

If you would be interested to hear more, I can possibly assist.

Regards

A.

Dorset

He followed this up on May 31st.

Neil,

It's difficult to know what you might not already know!

Are you aware, for example, that at the first Creditors' Meeting in London in late Oct 2019, Finbarr O'Connell, the team leader for the Administrators, addressed the meeting and said that there was roughly £100 million unaccounted for. We have repeatedly asked for that statement to be explained, but it never has been.

We have long suspected that quite a lot of the proceeds of sales went offshore, we think through inflated agent sales commissions. For example, we believe that some of these may have been as high as 30-35%. I know for a fact that the Director of the agent company in Malaysia that we dealt with, was proud of the fact that he had spent time at the Group First head office near Burnley in the early days (2015) and expressed to me that he was a Director of Park First's Asian subsidiary.

It would not take much imagination to see how this kind of setup could work to hide some of the sale proceeds offshore. Simply pay the "Agent" over the odds in commissions on the understanding that he forwards 50% (or so) of the fees to offshore accounts belonging to the proprietors.

We have often asked ourselves why the SFO did not get involved, but of course it is virtually impossible to find out if they had a look at this case or not.

Not sure if this is an angle you have pursued?

Regards

A.

Store First hit headlines after a client of Carey Pensions raised concerns with the investment. Carey Pensions advised Russell Adams to invest into the storage pods through a SIPP. He was introduced by a Spain-based unregulated introducer. Adams invested £50,000 into the pods in July 2012. His investment is now worthless.

In marketing videos posted on YouTube, investment claims were also made offering "a guaranteed return of 8% in the first two years, rising to 10 percent in years three and four." Some investors who directed their pensions to Store First said that the returns promised by the company were not correct.

Former sales agents for Jackson Francis told the BBC they were instructed by their immediate supervisors to lie about returns to get clients to invest. They admitted forging documents and also said they had witnessed other staff forging client signatures on documents. One sales agent told the BBC he saw staff ticking a box on forms indicating clients were OK with a high level of risk even though the question had not been asked of them.

In September 2014, the Self-Storage Association of the United Kingdom had warned investors that there were inaccuracies in Store First marketing material, alerting them to potential risks.

During a two-year period, Store First owner Toby Whittaker paid £33 million in commission to Transeuro Worldwide Holdings Ltd., a Gibraltar-based financial lead-generation services company that is believed to have funded the Liverpool-based Jackson Francis which is now in liquidation.

Jackson Francis acted as a sales agent for Store First. According to Whittaker, he and his company weren't responsible for the tactics used by the sales firm. "My company's sales agents are not employed to give financial advice; they are employed to explain the product, not to advise whether [it] is suitable for an individual's investment portfolio," he said.

On October 7th a winding up petition was filed against Transeuro, aiming to force the company into liquidation. The Transeuro website went offline, displaying only a note that said the site was undergoing maintenance. Interestingly, Transeuro was controlled by Mike Talbot, identified as a friend of Whittaker and the former co-director of Store First Midlands Ltd. Whittaker and Talbot previously operated Dylan Harvey, a property-investment company that went out of business while owing investors millions.

When eventually tracked down Talbot said he had no management or control of Jackson Francis and couldn't comment on the allegations.

With its base in Padiham, England, Store First has 12 self-storage facilities in England, mostly in the northwest region, and one in Scotland. The company's model blends traditional self-storage units with full business amenities for small enterprises, including use of P.O. boxes, free Wi-Fi and private meeting rooms.

A Petition to wind up Store First was lodged on May 18th, 2017. The company initially resisted the application until 30th April 2019 when it was wound-up in the High Court in the public interest by consent between the company and the

Secretary of State for the Department for Business, Energy and Industrial Strategy.

It's worth noting that Store First was promoted by former Top Gear presenter Quentin Willson, who appeared in a company video saying that he was always on the lookout for a good investment "like a guaranteed 8% in the first two years and up to 10% in years three and four".

However, in December 2019 it was reported that the freeholds, assets and goodwill associated with all Store First sites had been transferred to Store First Freeholds Ltd and Pay Store Ltd, businesses wholly owned by Jennifer Whittaker, wife of Store First CEO Toby Whittaker. A spokesman for the liquidators (The Official Receiver) said: "As liquidator of Store First and the associated companies, the Official Receiver has a duty to realise the assets in the interests of the creditors. The sale of the freehold, associated assets and goodwill of the 15 storage centres to Store First Freeholds Limited, as well as the sale assets of SFM Services Limited to Pay Store Limited, represented the best outcome for creditors." Really?

The deal means that investors may never be able to recover their money. They have been told they can surrender their storage pod and their liability for business rates, but no payment would be issued in return. In effect, their investment would be written off and you may well ask how that is fair and just. Store First has also given an undertaking not to market or sell storage pods to investors. However, this is little comfort to those who have already invested.

There is still an ongoing investigation into the cause of the collapse of Store First, according to the Insolvency Service. Over £200m was invested in Store First from UK pension funds and elsewhere, according to the Government's solicitor in the winding up case.

Store First were seemingly operating an Unregulated Collective Investment Scheme and that's very much FCA territory but the matter was led and prosecuted by the Department for Business, Energy and Industrial Strategy (BIS). Mr Whittaker's company, we are reliably told by a government solicitor acting in the winding up of it, received over £200m in investment from UK pension funds and private investors. On liquidation all the storage sites were sold back to him (for an as yet undisclosed sum). No refunds of investments have been made by either Mr Whittaker or his company.

Store First isn't the only problem Whittaker has on his plate.

In 2016 the FCA made its first intervention with Park First, another of Mr Whittaker's stable of companies, stopping the operation and promotion of the car parking scheme. As a result, the scheme was restructured, and investors were offered the chance to get their initial investment back or move into a different scheme. However, the operation proved to be uneconomic, and the companies involved in running the scheme entered into administration in July 2019.

In October 2019 the FCA began proceedings against Park First Limited, its senior managers, including its chief executive officer and a number of other companies connected to the Park First group. The proceedings sought compensation orders in favour of investors in respect of losses suffered in the Park First scheme.

The FCA alleged the Park First scheme involved an illegal collective investment scheme established to operate car park investments using funds from members of the investing public. The scheme raised approximately £230 million from 4,500 investors.

The regulator also alleged that the scheme was promoted to the public using false or misleading statements. The defendants made statements to the effect that investors could realistically expect returns of 10% in years 3 and 4 of their investment and 12% in years 5 and 6. The FCA alleged the defendants had no proper basis for these statements and that they were false or misleading. Park First also suggested that the investments were worth 25% more than the price for which they were being sold, based on independent valuations. However, they were aware that the valuations were based on unrealistic returns.

The FCA asked the Court to order the defendants to pay a just sum to the FCA to then distribute among the investors who have suffered loss as a result of Park First's alleged contraventions.

The FCA were also seeking a declaration that the schemes were collective investment schemes and that the defendants had unlawfully established, operated and promoted them (or were knowingly concerned in establishing, operating and promoting them), and had made false or misleading statements and impressions about the schemes. Injunctions to restrain the defendants from doing the same again were also requested.

The FCA's proceedings have been brought against chief executive, Toby Scott Whittaker, director John Slater and a number of companies involved or connected to the scheme, including Park First Limited, Harley Scott Residential Limited (previously known as Park First Glasgow Limited), Park First Skyport Limited, Paypark Limited, Help-me-park.com Limited and Group First Global Limited.

We can see then, that the FCA initially intervened in 2016 and issued proceedings in October 2019.

In July 2021 the FCA secured a conditional agreement with Park First in those proceedings. It was stated at the time that the agreement should see a further £25 million made available for compensation to investors on top of the £33 million already secured by the FCA out of the proceeds of the sale of the car park at Luton airport. However, the agreement is conditional on Park First investors approving Company Voluntary Arrangements (CVAs) in respect of these companies, which will give them a say about whether these arrangements and the conditional agreement are acceptable.

If the arrangements are approved, the defendants, including Mr Whittaker, will consent to orders that they breached section 19 of the Financial Services & Markets Act, 2000 by operating a collective investment scheme without being authorised by the FCA as required – which is of course a criminal offence. This admission only applies to the FCA's case. If the investors do not approve the arrangements and the conditional agreement, the FCA's proceedings against the defendants will continue.

Mark Steward, Executive Director of Enforcement and Market Oversight at the FCA said: "The agreement, if approved, represents a better outcome in the proceedings for investors than could have been achieved through continued legal action, given the financial position of the parties. It also gives investors the final say on the merits of the conditional agreement."

It is thought that Mr Whittaker will need to realise most of his assets to pay the sum of £25 million, which will be paid in instalments on the sale of the assets. If any instalment is unpaid, he has agreed not to contest the debt for the purpose of any bankruptcy proceedings brought by the FCA.

You'll recall that the FCA remit is to ensure that consumers get a fair deal. Toby Whittaker's companies have taken around £430m from pension funds and investors in just two schemes and in real cash terms agreed to repay a fraction of this in instalments. It's not surprising then, that many of the investors who have lost significant sums to the benefit of Toby Whittaker

127

are now thinking that the Financial Conduct Authority are failing in their endeavours to protect them.

It is possible that in recognition of investor sentiment the FCA, in April 2022 announced the launch of a new strategy to improve their handling of complaints:

FCA April 2022

"The FCA has launched a new strategy to improve outcomes for consumers and in markets throughout the UK.

As the FCA's remit is broad and growing, the three-year strategy prioritises resources to prevent serious harm, set higher standards and promote competition.

The regulator will also, for the first time, hold itself accountable against published outcomes and performance metrics.

A key focus of the strategy is shutting down problem firms, which do not meet basic regulatory standards.

The FCA is recruiting 80 employees to work on the initiative, which will protect consumers from potential fraud, poor treatment and create a better market.

In the development of the strategy, the FCA has calculated that for every pound spent on its operations, consumers and small businesses benefit by at least £11.

The regulator has also considered the rising cost of living, which could drive greater demand for credit products and lead consumers to look for new ways to manage and make more of their money.

The FCA will continue to work closely with the Government and Bank of England in response to the war in Ukraine.

The strategy builds on activities launched last July, when Nikhil Rathi, chief executive of the Financial Conduct Authority, committed the regulator to become more innovative, assertive and adaptive and transform the FCA into a data-led platform that can face the threats and opportunities of the future.

This approach led to the FCA reforming the general insurance market, saving consumers an expected £4.2bn over 10 years; leading the transition from LIBOR; helping small businesses claim £1.3bn against business interruption insurance cover; bringing its first ever criminal prosecution under anti-money laundering regulations, with NatWest fined £264m; and protecting consumers from scams by preventing unauthorised firms from advertising financial products on Google.

Rathi said: "Our new strategy enables the FCA to respond more quickly to the rapidly changing financial services sector. It will give us a foundation to continuously improve for the benefit of our stakeholders, and respond swiftly to economic and geopolitical developments."

It remains to be seen whether this "new strategy" makes any difference but there are already investors who feel that most of the regulators in this arena have achieved little or nothing on their behalf. Colin Rimmer is one of them. I received the following (unedited) email from him on June 3rd, 2022.

Message*: Hi Neil, We talked on the phone previously about the authorities burying fraud cases that they don't want to have to compensate. I know si much more now and believe that I can evidence corruption by multiple authorities - i.e. It being policy to bury significant fraud cases. I am a victim of several CIS's. e.g. Park First, MBi / NPD hotels, Alpha Properties. The most disturbing case though is the Ecohouse fraud. It is a fraud that the SRA covered up because it didn't want to have to compensate victims when insurance indemnity was ultimately declined for solicitor's involvement in fraud. The Met Police surreptitiously halted their investigation in 2017 when the lead investigator suddenly and unexpectedly left the case. They keep telling investors that they are still investigating, but really they are just treading water waiting for us to either give up or die. They have been investigating for 10 years now. There has been considerable collusion between the Met Police and the SRA, with the Met Police assisting the SRA to conceal solicitors dishonesty and to deny compensation through their compensation scheme. I firmly believe that the Government civered up the Ecohouse fraud because there is a former Tory Councillor at its centre and a Knight of the Realm is also* involved, as well as being the father of Clare Taman, one of the fraudulent solicitor partners who released hundreds of clients funds to non existent developments. In General I believe that the wretched Government doesn't want to have to fund criminal prosecutions against fraud perpetrators, and that is why only 1 in 700 frauds are criminally prosecuted in the UK. I have never managed to get any interest from the media in several years. There is a huge scandal and betrayal taking place, but nobody is listening. Can you help in that regard? Kind Regards, Colin Rimmer

A little later that day Colin emailed again:

A1 Alpha and MBi / NPD are both under investigation by the SFO. I submitted a controversial report to the SFO regarding Ecohouse, citing that some authorities had acted corruptly by trying to bury a fraud, but they just ignored my submission.

It concerns me greatly that Suella Braverman is the Attorney General and that the SFO reports to her. She has a constituent impacted by the Ecohouse fraud, but never lifted a finger to assist when requested. Several campaigns were targeted at her and another 140 MPs with constituents impacted by the fraud. When concerns were raised about the SRA perverting justice in the Ecohouse case, she just responded by saying that legal service regulation was independent of Government ; something that I happen to believe is a patent falsehood.

Given the contempt that she demonstrated towards her constituent regarding a significant fraud, it seems wholly

131

inappropriate for the SFO to be reporting to her, and I have grave concerns that she is influencing which cases the SFO investigates.

I believe that what I have unearthed during the last 7½ years of research exposes a culture of the Government and its agencies all vested in concealing rather than criminally prosecuting fraud. There are so many sub stories to tell about the various agencies.

Kind Regards,

Colin Rimmer

NB. You can read Suella Braverman's full response in the appendices.

Hi Neil,

Thank you for your message.

Yes, I am happy to be quoted as a significant victim of the Ecohouse fraud ~£140,000.

It isn't just the funds defrauded from 900 unsophisticated investors, it's the almost 8 years that I have spent fighting to get justice and redress against the fraud.

The SRA refused a grant of compensation before the Ponzi fraud was proven in court. The Met Police halted their investigation back in 2017, just as the investigating officer was about to take "Direct Police Action" against the solicitor perpetrators (his words). He then suddenly and unexpectedly left the case. I believe that the MoJ asked the Met Police to drop it, but why?

Was it to protect (a) former Tory Councillor ?

Was it to protect .... the father of solicitor partner Clare Taman?

Were other Tory officials involved?

Or is the Tory Government deliberately influencing regulatory authorities and the Police to conceal fraud cases because the Government does not want to have to fund criminal prosecutions?

One thing I can promise you - justice is being subverted. I am confident that this is a significant scandal with multiple authorities acting to conceal fraud rather than bring prosecutions. It is all down to money.

Kind Regards,

Colin

On Sunday 19th June 2022 I received the following email from an investor based in the Philippines together with his permission to quote it verbatim.

I am quite happy to share my details, I am from Wales, I am a "Chartered Quality Professional", i.e. I have made my career in an occupation that essentially implements clear and visible control systems to deliver what is expected.

I have lived and worked overseas since 1991 in professional roles in massive multimillion $ infrastructure construction projects for Governments and Major industries, with International companies, at last count working and living in 10 different countries. Some of the countries I have worked are rife with corruption (and scams), but with such global experience with Quality Management and Assurance systems for so long, I have always been cautious with investment, and always held a firm belief that the way the rules and courts seem to be in the UK, major scams and lack of legal support just cannot regularly happen in the UK - How wrong I was.

As happened, my father passed away in Wales 2018. With no intent to live back in the UK, with my siblings we sold up my father house, the home I grew up in. From the proceeds, with no urgent need for finance for my overseas life/home, I looked around for something to keep the inherited money in Wales, to perhaps use for holidays and to leave as a "legacy" for my two Welsh born (and living children). I found the Afan Valley scheme, researched it, watched all the shiny promotional videos such as this Afan Valley Adventure Resort - Press Event - YouTube and so I took the plunge.

Through a seemingly reputable Investment company over in Asia that sells property and investments in the UK and elsewhere, I bought into the Afan Valley scheme. So confident everything was above board and the project had "no chance" of failure as it was Government and Peter Moore OBE backed etc, I invested, and I even contacted the UK tax office to advise that as a 'Non-resident', I would 'after' the Afan Valley project was built (and my lease to rent the room to the developer signed), start to generate income from 2022, and so would became an 'overseas based landlord', with I assumed need for a tax return on UK earnings.

Everything from my side for the purchase was carried out professionally and legally by myself using the developer solicitor, and so the money left my bank. With my use of the inheritance from sale of my father house, I felt very happy to be keeping the money in something to benefit a part of my original 'home' country, Wales. I was also looking forward to spending holidays with my Welsh children there, with the promised returns on leasing the room to the Developer, secondary in my thoughts, but reportable to the UK tax office. And here I am now.

So, I was lulled into investing GBP50,000 as 'part' payment for a hotel room in the proposed "Treetops hotel" in the Afan Valley project and fell for the Welsh Assembly backed scheme hook line and sinker, using a UK bank and UK solicitor for my purchase, and confident it was a wise investment that could not fail.

When the development went into administration, I was amazed, but confident my money, or least part of it would be returned to me in due course. Some 3 (or is it 4) years later, I have not received back even 1 pound of my money. The way it has been dealt with leaves me furious with how unprofessionally it has been handled by the Courts, the official Administrator, the Authorities, the Welsh Assembly, and the UK Government - a huge scam, many people such as myself have been robbed in broad daylight. As I see and understand it -

- *The original backers of the scheme (Welsh Assembly, Gavin Woodhouse, Peter Moore OBE etc) appear to have crawled back into their holes and are hidden away laughing.*

- *The official Administrator seems to have done nothing to recover my money, even the solicitor they advised me to use declined to add me to his client base as he was too busy !*

- *The perpetrator of the scheme 'Gavin Woodhouse' seems to be living freely in a mansion, rolling in money, under investigation by the SFO, but still walking freely - instead of being locked up with all his assets sold to repay investors ?*

- *The Afan Valley project land, design and even original development plan has incredibly been sold on, and once again is being backed and supported by the councils where the land is, without anything coming back to me - one of the people who put money on the table to get the original scheme built ! Oh, the 'official Administrator I believe has claimed for over a million pound in his fees, after doing nothing I am aware of to get my money back.*

- *It seems the new 'developer' of the scheme, some mob called 'Wildfox' (with Peter Moore OBE still one of the Directors) are using a merchant bank umbrella to take the Afan Valley scheme forward - on my quick check, it appears some of the capital to be used has a distinct Russian connection, but does anyone care these days ?*

The whole situation from start to current time seems to have been well planned to lure investors, and then leave them high and dry with no easy route to recover their money, and no visible support from Courts or the Government. Shame on the UK, a great shame for the UK legal system to show such incompetence. Am I qualified to make such statement, Yes, I have made a successful career in ISO 9000 Quality Management systems, to ensure controls are developed and implemented to control massive major projects and stop these things happening.

I have tried (and remain trying) various angles, social media chat groups, UK solicitors and ideas to try and recover my money, if I had finance I would dearly like to get a class action to sue the Welsh Assembly Government office for backing it, Peter Moore OBE for backing it (and still being part of the scam version 2 being promoted), and if there was a fund to get Gavin Woodhouse with a noose around his neck I would gladly donate. The whole scenario has left me with a total distrust of the UK courts and legal system, and it goes without saying that I will never invest in anything in the UK again, the whole scenario is a total disgrace, my faith in the UK has gone.

In the meantime, the SFO investigating Gavin Woodhouse don't want to talk to me as I am not a UK resident, even though the money I used for the purchase originated in the UK from a house sale, never left a UK bank and was paid to the developer through a UK solicitor -- so why does my living overseas make a difference ?

Quite laughable also, HM tax office have mailed me several times telling me I need to do a tax return, and if I do not they will fine me - I have told them (and got an automatic receipt) that as a Non-Resident since 1991, the only reason I re-registered with them was due to potential tax on rental income of the room I bought in Afan Valley scheme - and that they should know that never happened. So as for a tax return and a fine - perhaps I will do it when HM Government and legal system help to get my money back from their backed scheme, and not before.

For information, I left the UK to work overseas in 1991, and overseas I remain, working in Philippines, with home base in Taiwan, I invest in numerous funds, and the only one that has left me furious is the "Welsh government Assembly" backed Afan Valley Project. A huge scam, by developer and all the backers, many of whom I pray Karma deals a massive blow to in the future, we can only but hope.

On June 18th, 2022, I emailed Mr. Skates.

From: Neil Bromage <neil@neilbromage.com>
Sent: 18 June 2022 11:56
To: Skates, Ken (Aelod o'r Senedd | Member of the Senedd) <Ken.Skates@senedd.wales>
Subject: Northern Powerhouse Developments Afan Valley

Dear Mr Skates,

You will see below that I'm writing a book about unregulated collective investment schemes in which Northern Powerhouse Developments features.

I have been contacted by a number of investors who are, to say the least, unhappy that you backed the Afan Valley project on behalf of the Welsh government. They claim that your support gave credibility to the scheme and was a significant factor in their investments. As you will appreciate, these people have lost significant sums of money, hence the level of anger amongst them.

139

As I'm dealing with this in the book, details of which you will find below, I would appreciate your comments in response to the investor's claim that your support for the scheme induced their investment.

Kind regards,

Neil

Ken Skates responded on Monday 20th June 2020.

Hi Neil,

Many thanks for your message. I'd be grateful if you could just elaborate more. I visited the site once and was recorded talking about how the project could offer positive change for the area and about how Bear Grylls being part of it was exciting. Many other public servants and journalists gave positive impressions of the vision and I understand the project has been given planning permission this year. My sentiments related to the vision of an adventure park in the valley, not to Northern Powerhouse's investment model. Was my visit to the site misused by Northern Powerhouse in their approach to investors?

Best wishes, Ken

I was a little disappointed by the MP's lack of understanding of what I thought were my clear words and so responded accordingly on Tuesday 21st June:

Dear Mr Skates,

Thank you for your email. I had hoped that my initial email was self-explanatory but for the sake of clarification perhaps you would respond to the investor's claim that support given by yourself, and the Welsh government gave credibility to the scheme and was a significant inducement to them to make investments.

Many thanks.

Kind regards,

Neil

Ken Skates then passed me on to the Welsh Assembly Head of News who said,

From: Simon.Jenkins@gov.wales <Simon.Jenkins@gov.wales>
Sent: 22 June 2022 12:34
To: neil@neilbromage.com

Subject: RE: Northern Powerhouse Developments Afan Valley

Hi Neil.

Ministers visit a wide range of organisations and businesses in the course of their official duties, including projects which might have the potential to be of economic benefit to Wales, such as the one in question. A ministerial visit is certainly not an endorsement of the viability of a particular project as an investment opportunity and ministers are careful not to give any such impression. As in other areas, potential investors need to rely on their own due diligence.

Hope this clarifies the position – and happy for you to use the above as a formal response from a Welsh Government spokesperson.

Kind regards

Simon.

Simon Jenkins

Head of News / *Pennaeth Newyddion*

First Minister's Official Spokesman / *Llefarydd y Prif Weinidog*
Welsh Government
Llywodraeth Cymru

Tel – 03000 25 8786
Mob - 0779 261 8138
Email - simon.jenkins@gov.wales

When pressed further Simon Jenkins refused to add anything to his initial statement. Investors will no doubt draw their own conclusions from this.

CHAPTER 8

Collateral Damage

It may all have started nearly twenty years ago with Guest
Invest but the last fifteen years have seen hundreds of illegally
structured hotels, student accommodation blocks and care
homes go down the drain. What looks like a great idea to a
developer is then dragged down into a murky pool of greed,
excess and ultimately manipulation when the first one is
completed.

It`s almost inevitable; "We`ve just made two million quid on
this, lets do another one, now! The need to invest at least some
of that "profit" into the development is quickly outweighed by
the desire for a Ferrari or a villa in Marbella. In some cases,
private jets and yachts also featured on the shopping lists of
corrupt developers.

One of the more difficult aspects to understand about many
of these failures is that they were failing a long time before they
finally collapsed. Moreover, the industry that supports all of this
unlawful activity often knows about the problems before they
become apparent to the wider world. One sales agent based in
Manchester told me that there were problems with the Signature

Living brand years before it went into administration because investors he had sold units to had not been paid. Another individual informed me that investors had issued court proceedings for recovery of unpaid rents due from Signature Living.

Signature Living was established by Lawrence Kenwright, Rumour and legend has it that Kenwright is related to the longstanding Everton Football Club chairman and theatre impresario William (Bill) Kenwright CBE. I've personally been told that Lawrence Kenwright is either Bill's brother, nephew or son. However, according to my friendly professional genealogist and family historian there is no connection whatsoever to be found. The very likeable theatre magnate may well be relieved.

In an interview for Trailblazer, a website which appears only to have been launched in 2022, Lawrence Kenwright was asked if he could remember when he first thought his business was in trouble:

"I'd say it began when I decided to sell 30 James Street and the Shankly to raise funds for further expansion. Both 30 James Street and the Shankly were fractional investor models, and the Shankly's investors were coming to the end of their term. I'd already repaid the 30 James Street investors, and they saw a 55% ROI. The idea was to kill two birds with one stone. Raise funds to expand our portfolio and pay Shankly's investors back. I settled on a deal with Savills to sell the Shankly and 30 James

Street for a total of £48 Million. We had a buyer and were almost across the line when Brexit boiled over, and Parliament was suspended. Prorogation will do it every time!

He continues:

Sterling fell, global investors became nervous and hit the pause (He probably meant "panic") *button, and just like that, the deal I had put in place fell through. That's when I first thought there could be trouble ahead. Many of Shankly's investors were foreign nationals, and they were no longer sure of the UK's prospects as an FDI haven. Brexit unsettled them, and they wanted to withdraw their funds in a hurry. It was a matter of timing; I was not in a position to honour their returns on investment immediately as the Savills deal had fallen through. We are talking about large sums of money, and for some of my investors, it was all the money they had. Their investments were their nest eggs, and I know first-hand, the thought of losing all you have will make you sick with worry.*

If you're overly sensitive, you can probably feel his pain!

What the investors did not know was that when the Savills deal fell by the wayside, I'd immediately begun looking to put another arrangement in place. One of the largest privately held funds in Europe wanted to buy into Signature Living in a 50/50 deal. Again, I was a whisker away from signing off when one of my investors Thomas Scullion, was interviewed by the Liverpool Echo. The headline of that hit piece read, "If I don't get my money back, I'm finished". Unfortunately, that headline was

146

enough to scupper the deal. Within hours of the piece going to press, I got a phone call from the CEO of my future, the negative press had caused them to rethink, and they withdrew. So you see, there had been little fires everywhere leading up to being placed in administration, but I'd been working tirelessly to put them all out. That deal would have seen Signature secure a £200 million funding pot. The Shankly's investors would have been repaid, and our expansion would have continued. I was so close to avoiding the situation I found myself in, but that's the way it played out.

It has to be said that it was a very, very good interview and Mr Kenwright said all the right things and comes across as a really caring chap. But in his desire to explain that Brexit, the fall of Sterling and global investors becoming nervous and wanting to withdraw their funds in a hurry were the real problem he's slightly missed the point. That is, that he was, and it appears still is running an illegal unregulated collective investment scheme. As for Brexit and Parliament being suspended being causes of his business teetering on the brink Kenwright has conveniently failed to mention a number of things and some of those "little fires" were already burning and suggest that his business hit the skids quite some time before he would have us believe.

What follows are unedited copies of postings taken from the *Signature Living Investments Scam* Facebook page which has now been "archived".

Nov 2019:

I have an investment with Signature Capital that should have paid out yesterday and hasn't been. In the week before I have emailed, left voicemails and even messaged Katie to ask for an update but have had no response. I didn't get any kind of communication from Signature that the investment wouldn't be paid on time - absolute radio silence. Is anyone else in the same boat?

Also, I just tried to post this question on the 'Signature Capital Invest' FB page. It let me type the question and hit 'Post'. but then didn't appear as a post.

Oct 31st, 2019:

As I keep my eye on The Gazette publications, not a month goes by without investors like us filing petitions for Winding-Up Orders on Signature - like one of this most recent ones
https://www.thegazette.co.uk/notice/3132036

This seems to be the only way to get any money from them, unfortunately.

Sep 4th, 2019:

Apparently we, Shankly investors, are in even bigger trouble that we thought we were: **https://www.rightmove.co.uk/commercial-property-for-sale/property-84094508.htm**

Will forward this to the BBC team - just in case they have not dug this out already.

July 28th, 2019:

Signature Living Hotel Ltd has an outstanding debt of £89,439, for which no summons has yet been issued.

May 11, 2019:

Investors in a multi-million-pound luxury hotel group said they have been through "a nightmare" trying to get money from the company.

They described months of delays and unanswered calls or emails to the Liverpool company, Signature Living.

The BBC has spoken to six investors, from the UK, Ireland, Singapore and Taiwan, who said they were owed money.

Company boss Lawrence Kenwright, who is considering running for mayor of Liverpool, said everyone would be paid.

https://www.bbc.com/news/uk-england-merseyside-48152236

Mar 2019:

This is the comment I posted under this article:
https://www.dailymail.co.uk/.../Hotel-firm-Signature...

Each room in every hotel named here - The Shankly Hotel, George Best Hotel, Coal Exchange Hotel in Cardiff – has an investor behind it, a person like me or, maybe you, who had

been saving for their old age and one day was found by a
Signature salesman or their agent. That was the day when
Signature got our money and promised to pay us a guaranteed
rent on OUR rooms in those hotels – "quarterly in arrears",
that is what our contracts say. However, as soon as Signature
got our money... for most of us it is now "yearly in arrears"
and no hope of getting it ever. If you google "signature
investments" and read what people say in Google reviews or
check out "signature investments Trustpilot" you will get the
picture.

You as a newspaper should be ashamed of yourselves for
publishing such promo materials without researching into the
background.

Apr 2019

UPD. Contacted BBC Watchdog today.

Will be sending report to SFO and other bodies later this week.
My co-investor is planning to go to the national press through
his own connections.

Next port of call will be http://www.actionfraud.police.uk. *I am*
going for the kill. And the more people will follow, the surer the
kill will be.

But perhaps one of the most damning is the most recent:

Oct 2020:

I first dealt with SL as an estate agent 6 years ago the agency I worked for was given Daniel house to sell I sold a few units and at the time I thought they was great with the swimming pool on the roof etc!

Can't believe how bad the finished product is now and I feel so bad I even sold those units all that time ago. I know people can't even sell them as they cannot get any information from the leaseholder to complete a sale!

It makes me sick how this man can do a BBC program and show his face to the world as some kind of genius. He knows every loop hole to avoid jail but he's basically stolen millions of pounds of people all over the world.

As victims I don't know how it must feel to watch this show. I own an estate agents in Liverpool now and I am now carful what developers to work with due to people him.

There was a huge covid break out in the Shankly a few weeks ago and Lawrence reported nothing and told all the events to carry on as normal as he didn't want to close down the hotel with him just getting new investors on board to save that hotel! - shows what Type of man he is doesn't care about anyone but himself!

I spoke with the echo they said they wasn't reporting anything at all to do with the show out of respect for the victims which I applaud 👏👏👏

It is clear from the dates of these posts that Kenwright`s problems were present before the date he suggests they started.

This type of behaviour is not exactly uncommon amongst the developers of these big schemes, though it should also be said that Lawrence Kenwright`s Signature brand, whilst sizeable in its own right isn`t one of those big schemes.

Northern Powerhouse Developments (NPD) is without doubt a big scheme having taken in an estimated £80m from approximately 1300 small investors. David Niven, a partner in a leading law firm said at the time of the failure of NPD that it was "one of the biggest collapsed property schemes of its type they had come across".

Northern Powerhouse Developments was headed up by Gavin Woodhouse. At the point of writing Woodhouse is being investigated by the Serious Fraud Office.

Whilst my head was still buried in the legislation, I watched the rise of Woodhouse and NPD with interest, particularly as he began to build not only his "empire" but also the board of directors appointed to help him achieve his goals. Having a strong and impressive collection of directors is always helpful to a company. If those directors are high profile individuals, even better, particularly if appointed to create an image.

So, I was particularly interested when Peter Moore OBE joined the board in January 2017 as non-executive chairman of leisure, which of course, suggests that not only was NPD growing but also developing different divisions, or what some might call lofty ambitions.

Mr Moore certainly came to NPD with impeccable credentials as the former Centre Parcs managing director. He had also been at Alton Towers, Chill Factore indoor ski village in Manchester and had served two terms on the board of the national tourism authority in England. He received his OBE in 1996 for services to tourism.

He was subsequently joined on the "board" in July 2017 by another heavyweight from the world of leisure and hospitality. Richard Lewis was the former boss of Best Western Hotels GB and chief executive of Dubai based Landmark Hotels, the operator of nine establishments across the Middle East. He had also previously worked for the Savoy Hotel Group, Forte and Le Meridien.

Woodhouse had clearly chosen well, but he hadn`t quite finished. In May 2018 he enticed Russell Kett, chairman of the London office of global hospitality consultancy HVS to join the "board". Kett is another hugely experienced figure in hospitality. HVS website describes him as, "40 years' specialist hotel consultancy, **investment and real estate experience**, focused on providing valuation, feasibility, **shared ownership**, property, brokerage, **investment**, asset management, strategy and related consultancy services, **advising** hotel, serviced apartments and hostel companies, **banks, developers and investors on all aspects** of their hospitality industry related

153

interests, throughout the EMEA region. Russell is a frequent writer, moderator and speaker on the international hotel industry, especially topics relating to hotel valuation, **investment**, marketing and finance." (Highlighting mine),

It is abundantly clear that all three men had impeccable CV's and experience and would together make a formidable team. However, as I watched each of these well documented appointments, I was left with one overriding thought; *why don't these guys realise NPD is running an illegal unregulated collective investment scheme?* They were, after all, very experienced businessmen, and moreover, property men.

Woodhouse clearly had an eye for choosing those who could help him reach his goals, but he also used them. When the appointments of all three of the above mentioned were announced to the media each one acknowledged that they were being appointed to the "board". We all know that this means the Board of Directors, those people who run the company and ensure everything is done properly. However, despite Richard Lewis's media announcement stating clearly that he was actually being appointed as chief executive none of these three men appears to have ever been registered as a director of any NPD companies. Whilst there's nothing wrong in having non-executives on a board the reality is that they have no control at all over the actions of the real owners of the company. In this instance, and as expert as each of these three men undoubtedly are, they were merely window dressing, mannequins designed to entice people in – and hand over their cash.

One of those who did just that was Vijay Devadoss, a retired NHS orthopaedic surgeon who paid £450,000 for nine rooms in Mr Woodhouse's Clifton Moor care home development in 2015. He was told that Clifton Moor would be operational and generating profits by 2018 but work at the site in Greater Manchester hasn't begun. Mr Devadoss told ITV News, "I was expecting a nursing home with 70 beds, so I'm really shocked to see that nothing has happened. If my wife was here, she would start to cry. I'm really upset but what else can I do? We were banking on [this] for our future. It is our real lifetime savings and pension for us. Because of this both of us have to rethink our plans and carry on working."

Woodhouse launched the Clifton Moor care home project in 2014 and raised £4 million from investors like Mr Devadoss. Between 2013 and 2015, he persuaded investors to stump up £16 million to finance the construction of four off-plan care homes. The Smithy Bridge care home near Rochdale was built but never opened, The Walsden Care Village scheme in Calderdale remains a timber yard and the Hawthorn Care Village in Burnley is still a disused school.

Woodhouse raised £5 million from investors to build the Hawthorn Care Village but he didn't own the land and Lancashire County Council told him that it wouldn't sell the land to him. He hadn't even submitted planning permission for a care home at the site despite telling investors he had.

Whilst all this was ongoing, and investors were trying to find out precisely where their money was Gavin Woodhouse was trying to raise money for his Afan Valley Adventure Resort in South Wales. Once more he needed a high-profile figure to provide credence and credibility.

The unfortunate victim this time was none other than TV personality and survival expert Bear Grylls OBE. Apart from being a genuinely decent guy Bear Grylls is an Honorary Colonel to the Royal Marines Commandos, the youngest ever UK Chief Scout, and the first ever Chief Ambassador to the World Scout Organization, representing a global family of some fifty million Scouts. Put simply, the man is something of a legend and it`s unfortunate that he was taken in by Woodhouse`s patter – but he clearly wasn`t alone.

Afan Valley Adventure Resort would have occupied 327 acres on which would be built ski slopes, zip wires, high wire, an aqua park, equestrian centre, mountain biking track, BMX track and skate park, plus a 100-bed hotel, spa, retail and restaurants plaza, the European HQ of the Bear Grylls Instructor's Academy, and parking for 800+ cars. There would also be 600 lodges.

What were investors getting for their money and what, precisely would they have owned? Interestingly, this is what Northern Powerhouse Developments (Holdings) Ltd, expressed in the notes to the 2017-18 accounts:

"It is the belief of the management of the group that the risks and rewards of ownership do not pass to lessees of the hotel rooms, as the group maintains control over the room operation, maintenance and insurance. In addition, the lessee receives fixed annual rental income and there is a fixed price for the group to buyback the room in the future. As such the transaction is treated as an operating lease for the group as lessor."

One commentator said that in this view, the investor does not acquire the physical asset for the stated number of years, but the right to a specified quantity of income from it and that this 'management belief' would also mean that the physical assets could be offered for sale without the agreement of investors. It may well be that this is what NPD hoped was the case but if a room is owned by an investor and their name is on the lease and registered at the Land Registry that investor owns that property however worthless it may be.

In the course of trying to develop his Afan Valley project Woodhouse never mentioned his struggling care home schemes to potential investors, but he did tell them that Jaguar Land Rover and Go Ape were "partners" on the project. These claims were made repeatedly in marketing material, newspaper articles, and in Woodhouse's planning submission to Neath Port Talbot Council.

Neath Port Talbot Council did grant conditional outline planning permission for the project. The council said it received a letter from Mr Woodhouse's solicitor, Metis Law, stating it held "contracts and commercial agreements" with Jaguar Land Rover and Go Ape and claimed that all partners were "legally and contractually engaged".

Not surprisingly, Jaguar Land Rover said that whilst it had held talks with Mr Woodhouse it was "not in any official partnership" and that "no commitment has ever been made" to the Afan Valley project. Go Ape mirrored this saying it was "interested in the project" but hadn't agreed terms and nothing had been signed. Someone is clearly misleading someone, somewhere.

In late June 2019 The Guardian newspaper and ITV News published the results of an undercover investigation into Woodhouse and NPD. Within a week the ship was going down and Peter Moore and Russell Kett jumped. The headline on this occasion referred to "advisers" quitting rather than directors. A change of tone that would no doubt be welcomed by those departing.

Peter Moore told the media that he had resigned because the allegation in the Guardian and ITV investigations were "causing understandable concern to many of the organisations involved in delivering the Afan Valley project."

However, Russell Kett claimed that he was embarrassed and concerned his professional integrity was being called into question. This is not at all surprising when you consider that Northern Powerhouse Developments (Holdings) – the company behind the Afan Valley resort, as well as 11 operational hotels – posted a £7m profit in the year to March 2018 and claimed its balance sheet had net assets of £11.2m. These figures would have been wiped out if it wasn`t for a £22m hike in the valuation of the hotels. The accounts, which were personally signed off by Woodhouse, state: "All hotels have been independently valued by HVS." However, in a statement issued to the Guardian and ITV News, Kett said: "In February 2018 the valuation division of HVS London issued a draft report on nine of NPD's hotels for their internal asset evaluation purposes only and to assist in their strategy initiatives; this was subject to a number of specific assumptions. "A final version of this draft report was never issued because of outstanding information relevant to the valuation conclusions. As we were effectively waiting for crucial information to assist our valuations, any figures used in any professional capacity cannot be endorsed by HVS."

In granting interim powers to accountancy firm Duff and Phelps to go into NPD ahead of formal administration orders the High Court Judge described the Woodhouse businesses as "thoroughly dishonest" and said that she was "entirely satisfied" that the court needed to take immediate action. She added that investors had paid money to Woodhouse in the belief that it was to be ring-fenced for a specific project but that "this was untrue".

It is thought that £15 million may have gone missing from the accounts of the Woodhouse companies.

It was in the early summer of 2019 when one of the biggest unlawful schemes collapsed. In fact, it was around the same time that I finally lifted my head out of the regulations and revealed to an open office that it was impossible to sell rooms in hotels, care homes and student accommodation blocks unless you are properly authorised by the FCA. It was the point at which, in a single afternoon, we put up the website for UCIS Advice Point, with no real understanding of where it might lead.

It initially led to no more than a handful of visits to the website. However, we did become the focus of a particular review site which claims to protect investors with information but whose powers of research fall well short of enabling accurate journalism.

Safe or Scam claim that they only investigate "scams" and yet also say clearly that they are "very experienced.........in recovering investments". This at least suggests much more than mere investigations but that they also assist investors to make claims which are then referred to and handled by solicitors – possibly through a company which is not associated with Safe or Scam. Their website was recently moved out of the UK and jurisdiction of the FCA. It is now based in New Mexico. Unfortunately, their "reporting" falls well short of the standards of good journalism and their modus operandi seems to be to shoot at anyone who may appear to be competition to their non-investigative activities. As well as targeting UAP they have maligned top solicitors who have worked tirelessly and successfully for claimant groups in this arena. As one respected lawyer said recently, "it's almost become a badge of honour to have Safe or Scam write about you". It is certainly true that much of what they wrote about UAP and me was not thoroughly researched and on one occasion they had clearly resorted to using confidential information obtained from Matthew Longworth in the form of an invoice, incorrectly but innocently sent from the wrong account. It also became clear to me when I met with insolvency practitioners, Quantuma, that a relationship already existed with Safe or Scam. SOS have also recently taken over the Bond Review website.

It became clear that Safe or Scam were merely on mission to close down UCIS Advice Point. In late 2021 the FCA wrote to UAP about their concerns that it should be regulated as claims management company. UAP wrote back at length and pointed out that all claims handled by UAP were in fact professional negligence claims and these are not covered by the regulations. That response was sent by email but according to the FCA not received by them even though we did not get a "failed to send" or similar message from our domain provider. As a result of the FCA not receiving our initial response they to us wrote again in more formal terms and included a "cease and desist" notice, which we immediately complied with, whilst responding to them again and including a copy of our original letter. On this occasion the correspondence was emailed and posted by way of recorded delivery. Six months later we eventually received a final response from the FCA. In short, they merely said that our website (which had been taken down six months ago) required a change to some wording, "…..the website will need to be re-drafted in order to set out the information referred to above in far more detail and in such a way that consumers are clear about their position should they wish to use the services offered by your firm". There is no suggestion that UAP needed to be regulated and the FCA`s final letter can be read in the Appendices. However, UCIS Advice Point has now changed its name to UCIS Helpline and operates exclusively under agreement with an existing and regulated claims management company in order that there can be no similar cries of "scam" from SOS.

One of those early visits to the website determined our direction clearly as we became intimately involved with A1 Alpha thanks to the assistance of an investor who was co-ordinating a large group of claimants in the failed scheme.

It is thought that there may be as many as two thousand investors in the Alpha scheme which appears to have raised as much as £150 million from small investors in about fifty different countries around the world. Over the next few months UCIS Advice Point was contacted by many of them thanks to the work of that lead investor.

On the 8th of February 2020 I wrote an article for the Financial Mail on Sunday about our lead investor`s experience of A1 Alpha following which we were deluged with enquiries on a variety of schemes. What followed was a sobering reminder of the shenanigans that goes on in this environment and that only one thing reigns. Duplicity.

Having pulled together a growing group of claimants we began a dialogue with a leading international law firm. A top 25 law firm to be precise, with a turnover of around £300 million. The people we dealt with really quite nice. Both partners in the firm and both very experienced in these types of claims.

We worked closely with the law firm for some months as we slowly pulled together an initial group of investors numbering around 250. They also introduced a funder into the mix in order that their own fees could be paid on an ongoing basis. The funder wanted to charge the investor as much as 40% of whatever they might recover. That was an amount we thought was too high and would deter investors from signing up to the scheme. The funder also wanted a much larger group of investors in order to make it viable for them. They set the group claim value at £30 million which would require around seven hundred and fifty investors to join the scheme, three times the number we had already introduced to them. Additionally, and at the eleventh hour the funders decided that UCIS Advice Point needed to be regulated by the FCA and it wasn't because all these claims are for professional negligence which is not covered by the regulations. As a result, months of work was dispatched to the dustbin as investors became nervous about the chances of the scheme even getting off the ground.

However, the work done by UCIS Advice Point meant that the relationship with investors and in particular the lead investor was still strong. The investors could see that UAP had done a lot of work for absolutely no return. The A1 Alpha scheme was hugely significant, particularly for those two thousand investors and someone needed to help them recover their losses.

As that deal unravelled and UAP were left wondering what to do next Matthew Longworth entered the fray. I had known Longworth for a few years but had never done business with him. Despite this, he had been in and out of our office on a regular basis and we also knew a number of people who knew him – at that point without detrimental comment. He had also previously asked us to meet with his friend and business associate Stuart Davies, a wealthy individual who lends money to, et al, property developers through his company A Shade Greener Finance Ltd. One of the companies he had lent money to was Shepherd Cox which operated hotels and storage facilities in a manner consistent with unlawful unregulated collective investment schemes and has largely now failed. It seemed Davies was concerned that he may not get his money back.

Longworth asked us to meet with him and Davies at the latter's office in Tankersley, South Yorkshire, where we spent a whole day educating Davies and his team about UCIS. But it was the start of the meeting that really sticks in my mind. Whether that's because Davies likes to stamp his personality on a meeting I'm not sure, but he did. He began by telling us his story of building up a fortune, retiring to Switzerland and then losing most of it in the banking crisis of 2008 before returning to the UK to make another fortune – about half a billion it seems - out of solar panels. That bit was impressive as I`ve huge respect for people who can overcome failure and go on to greater things. But he then slid a bank statement across the table showing a credit balance of about one hundred and twenty million pounds. That`s just one account he said. For some reason I`m reminded of the multi-millionaire owner of Patak`s Spices, a worldwide provider of Indian food. Kirit Pathak was a genuinely lovely guy and when I first interviewed him he offered to take my wife and I out to dinner at his favourite Indian restaurant. I was merely a journalist doing an interview for which he had already given up a significant amount of his time (along with two goodie bags of Patak`s produce) and he was still prepared to give up his evening to take me to dinner. Humble generosity personified.

As no one had commented negatively about Longworth at that time I saw no reason to steer clear of him. When the Alpha claim looked as though it was faltering, he told us that he could introduce the claims to Irwin Mitchell solicitors, and we entered into an arrangement which was something between a joint venture and a partnership. We had all the clients and Longworth had a solicitor ready to take them on.

Initially, that arrangement was verbal and made between me and Longworth. It was then set out in an agreement which Longworth never signed.

I've been around long enough to know that duplicity exists in most areas of business and I shouldn't therefore be surprised by it. Once the contact had been established with Longworth's solicitor pal, then at Irwin Mitchell solicitors (an established and otherwise reputable firm), UCIS Advice Point proceeded to gather together as many investors as possibly. Irwin Mitchell held a Webinar with investors to provide them with more information. I took part in that webinar as a member of the "team". I even had to provide clarification on a legal point that the solicitor was struggling to explain clearly. In the end, we pulled together around 250 investors.

It was now time to provide our complete database of all those clients, and others to Irwin Mitchell to enable them to make direct contact with them and begin the process of onboarding as clients. We gave Longworth access to our database, and he simply passed it on to the solicitor at IM.

The film director Billy Wilder said that hindsight is always 20/20, despite which I should probably have seen what was about to happen.

At this point Longworth has obtained everything needed to take this very substantial claim – c£15 million – forward. He's got access to all of our clients and is successfully manipulating the solicitor. He then says that neither I nor UCIS Advice Point can have any further communication with the solicitor at IM as they are not prepared to work with us due to "background issues". It is a fact that one of the partners in UAP was a former solicitor and subsequently struck off by the Law Society. He therefore resigned from the partnership.

At this point I became suspicious of Longworth's intentions, and he was of course, bankrupt at the time. Whilst he continued to maintain he would honour our agreement he also now wanted us to have that agreement with a third party and a new company set up just for this purpose with his "partner" Neil Gregory Duckworth, who in 2017 was bankrupted owing £4.6m. That company was XJS129 Ltd. Interestingly, whilst these Alpha claims have yet to be concluded there is currently (22nd June 2022) an active proposal to strike off that company at Companies House.

The lion's share of any money to be made in these claims will always be with the funders. Longworth recognised this and repositioned himself as the lender in the form of a newly incorporated limited company. KL Capital Ltd was established with his wife as the sole director, obviously due to his bankruptcy. She had no involvement whatsoever and was never present at any discussions. She subsequently resigned her directorship at a point following her husband's discharge from bankruptcy.

As a bankrupt Longworth should not have had the sort of funds that were going to be required to fund the solicitors - £3k per case he told us, and hence the reference to the £800K allegedly deposited with IM. However, he had already told us that the only person he could find who was interested in funding the claim was his friend Stuart Davies but that he wanted a 200% return. For every pound lent and returned he would therefore receive two more. Nice work if you can get it! I received an email from Neil Duckworth of Middle Barton Ltd in late 2021 confirming that monies already paid to solicitors totalled c£250K.

Despite Longworth's "instruction" I called the solicitor directly and asked him two simple questions; is it true that you don't want any direct contact with either me or UAP? Eventually, and a little reluctantly he said no. At a later date he went on to confirm in writing that he wanted a relationship with all of us. My second question related to Longworth's written assertion that he had placed £800,000 on deposit with Irwin Mitchell towards their fees. The solicitor also confirmed that this was not true.

By this time, Longworth's skeletons are falling out of cupboards as I became more aware of his background and how he had performed almost identical scams on others, one for as much as £1m and another for around £200K. Subject to how the claim develops and is eventually settled UAP's loss could easily amount to more than £1m.

Whatever the number was, most of those claims related to the A1 Alpha development at Scholars Green in Bradford but that was only one in a very long list of developments undertaken by A1 Alpha.

David Yang, a former fund manager from Taiwan who invested in the scheme, said he could not believe what had happened, adding he was unable to access the rooms he had bought leases on. "I spent £310,000 to buy four rooms in [the] UK . . . and now I even cannot have my keys," he said.

Some of the retail investors involved in the A1 Alpha scheme have put much of their life savings into it. One used the £52,000 lump sum she received on retiring early as a nurse on a lease at the scheme's Bradford site. When she went to visit the site, she was concerned that she was unable to see the room but was pacified by a salesperson saying to her, 'You really don't need to worry about your unit being tenanted, because even if your unit remains empty for 10 years, you will still be paid, because it is contractual." The investor, who suffers from ill health, said she had felt reassured by how she thought she was buying into a business rather than an individual property.

It probably doesn't need to be said but this is an all too familiar tale across the Alpha schemes just as it is with many others. So let's take a look at who was behind A1 Alpha.

In addition to acting as directors at A1 Alpha Properties (Leicester) Ltd, Derek Kewley and Nicholas Spence were also directors at the development companies. The day-to-day running of a number of the properties was originally handled by Mezzino Ltd, a separate company. Following a dispute Mezzino was replaced with Alpha Student Management, which was also run by Kewley and Spence. The two men then, were directors

169

of the development companies, the company that committed to pay investors a return, and, following the dispute, the service company, which was responsible for overseeing the day-to-day running of the buildings. A further director, Peter Sullivan, was appointed director of A1 Alpha Properties (Leicester) Ltd, in January 2018 and Kewley and Spence subsequently resigned.

In keeping with what seems to have become industry practice, the development companies actually sold the freeholds of each property to Premier Ground Rents Ltd. Those sales would raise further substantial income for Kewley and Spence. However, there must be a question over those freehold sales, particularly if they occurred after the individual rooms began to be sold.

The insolvent company A1 Alpha Properties (Leicester) Ltd, as well as paying returns to investors and receiving rents from students, also committed to pay ground rents and service charges. The investors had committed to pay these charges in turn when they bought the leasehold interest in a room. While the scheme was working, A1 Alpha Properties (Leicester) Ltd simply paid the fees directly, but because that company is now in administration, it cannot do so. Investors subsequently received emails asking them for payment of ground rents and service charges. In the case of the Bradford site, for example, payment was requested for ground rents of £125 and service charges of £367.46 per quarter and investors have been under pressure to make the payments themselves.

It's worth noting that across the scheme, the ground rents and high service charges outweigh incoming rents from students. £4.5m of rents were coming in annually, compared to £1.2m of ground rents and £3.9m of service charges.

Around £150m went into the Alpha scheme from as many as two thousand investors. The directors claim that the majority of this money was used for development, renovation, infrastructure, and was invested back into A1 Alpha. While they also resigned from that company and the management company, Kewley and Spence are still shown as directors of the developer companies which sold the rooms, and those companies are still "active" according to Companies House.

The marketing materials for the Stoke development claimed its location, close to Keele University and the University of Staffordshire, "ensures high demand in a thriving student city". I was born and spent my childhood in Stoke-on-Trent and despite not living there now I have lived back there and owned an estate agency in the heart of the area. Most of my extended family still live there and at least one went to Keele Uni` which is quite a long way from the centre of Stoke where the Alpha development is. Furthermore, both Keele and the University of Staffordshire have ample supply of good purpose-built student accommodation.

Kewley and Spence blame the competing supply for the schemes' difficulties. However, according to notes from the creditors meeting even if the property was fully let it would only bring in £10m income. Most of the sites offered returns of 10 per cent — meaning even maximum rents, as it currently stands, would not appear to be enough to pay the investors the amount in the contracts after accounting for costs. This is a common theme across all of these failed UCIS developments.

The developer prospectus listed fifteen sites and claimed that twelve of them were already "fully operational & 100% occupied". This amounted to 1,654 of the 2,216 units but occupancy rates were just over 50 per cent, as of February 2019. Another page on the prospectus was entitled "freeholds retained by the developer" when the freeholds were sold to another company by the directors.

In the wake of the failure a number of investors gathered together and instructed Trowers and Hamlin solicitors to instigate ex-parte proceedings to freeze all the worldwide assets of the directors and a number of companies. There were eleven defendants in all, including Andrew Crump.

Andrew John Leslie Crump was the sole director of Emerging Property Investments Limited, the marketing company responsible for sales of units in the Alpha schemes. He was also a co-director of Emerging Property Ltd. Both companies were defendants in the ex parte application to freeze assets.

In the skeleton argument presented to the court by the claimant investors they said that Crump knew that the representations made in the marketing material were false, or that he had no honest belief in them, or that he was reckless as to whether they were true, therefore causing those two companies to be liable in deceit. In his Judgment Mr Justice Calver said,

"There is evidence, therefore, before me that the fourth defendant was involved in the scheme from the start, and that this was a collaborative venture with the first and second defendants. The claimants also rely upon the fact that the Property Ombudsman found that there was no evidence to suggest that the fourth defendant had undertaken due diligence to ensure that all information presented in their marketing campaign was accurate and not misleading. The response of Mr Crump (the third defendant) to this was to deny this. However, the difficulty with his response is that he accepted that he was provided with the terms of the contractual documents (the lease agreements) before he, the fourth and fifth defendants started to sell the units. If that is so, one asks the question: why did he not seek to correct his sales literature, because these documents fundamentally diverged in very important respects? Indeed, it can also be seen that his company was actually responsible for providing draft contracts to investors and arguably misleading them on this point: see the email of 1st June 2018, to which I was referred. The documents put before me suggest that Mr Crump knew that the guaranteed rent was 10 only as secure as the financial standing of the underlessee. That is apparent from Emerging Property's email of January 2016, to which I was referred, where it is stated that it is the developers' asset base

173

which provides the security. But that appears to have been false. Mr Crump was at the very least, on a good arguable case basis, reckless as to whether or not this was true. Indeed, in one of Emerging Property's brochures there is a reference to competitors of Emerging Property signing contracts with SPVs, which is said to be not a secure method to adopt, precisely because those SPVs may subsequently have significant financial difficulties which render the investors' investments liable to be forfeited. In this case what was being said was that, in contrast, the investors had the security of the developers' strong financial standing to ensure that their investments were safe; whereas it is strongly arguable that Mr Crump would have known, having seen the relevant lease documentation which purported to give effect to the representations that had been made in the brochures, that that was not the case. From all of this, I consider that to a good arguable case standard it can be inferred that the third defendant knew that the representations were false, or at the very least elected not to confirm that the representations were true and that he was therefore reckless as to their truthfulness.

I agree .... that there is at least a good arguable case to say that Mr Crump must have known those statements to be false when they were made; or at least he must have been reckless as to their truth. In many cases it is clear that the contracts were not underwritten by the developers' large asset base, as was represented in the brochures; rather, the contracts, if underwritten at all, were underwritten by SPVs, whose financial

174

standing was not reliable, as indeed has transpired. There is a good arguable case that Mr Crump either knew that, or ought to have known that, in the light of the fact that he received the underlying lease documentation. I accordingly consider that there is a good arguable case that each of the defendants is guilty of deceit.

The world-wide freezing order was granted (and can be found in the Appendices) to the investors but just how much they have been able to recover is uncertain. Equally uncertain it seems is whether any of the monies recovered will go to the investors who fought for it or into the receiver's pot.

On September 29th, 2021, The SFO carried out coordinated raids on addresses connected with A1 Alpha. The SFO said that it suspects the Alpha-branded companies of fraudulently misleading investors into buying leaseholds for student accommodation in Leicestershire, Lancashire, Staffordshire, and West Yorkshire. The Green Park branded companies are also suspected of misleading investors. The SFO published a complete list of Alpha companies under investigation which appears at the end of this chapter.

Shepherd Cox (SC) have been mentioned more than once and as they present an interesting study into some of the relationships entwined in a number of these schemes it's worth taking a closer look at them. Whilst they were not large by NPD standards, they did at one point own at least sixteen hotels where the room sales will have seen them draw in around £40m in revenue.

They began life as an agent, and I first came across them when our friend Mike told us about the two hotels he and his partners were buying in Knutsford and Lymm. They had engaged Shepherd Cox to sell the rooms but the way in which this happened was probably unique in this area and was clearly driven by Shepherd Cox having an eye on the bigger prize and clearly not being content with remaining merely an agent.

Shepherd Cox sold the vast majority of rooms in the two Cheshire-based hotels in Singapore and many of the investors who bought rooms figured they were onto a good thing. They were lured by advertisements claiming, "guaranteed 24% net return over three years" and "109% guaranteed buyback".

One such investor, who wanted only to be known as "Nick" when interviewed by The Property Edge in Singapore, saw the advertisement about Ibis Warrington Lymm and attended the property seminar together with his wife. The returns dangled that day were even sweeter than what was advertised, with offers of 9% return a year and 115% buyback at the end of three years.

The price of a hotel room at Ibis Warrington Lymm was £94,500, which translated into about $200,000 then. "What convinced us to buy were the high returns, the assurance that it was a completed project and, more importantly, because of DWG [Dennis Wee Group], which we thought was a very

176

reputable marketing agency," says Nick. He signed the option to purchase and paid the booking fee of $4,000 (£2,000) on July 13.

As the advertisement had said, "Meet the developer", Nick was introduced to Lee Bramzell, founder, and director of Shepherd Cox, who made a presentation on the project that day. "They should have just told us the developer couldn't make it, but here is the marketing agent from the UK," says Nick. "Instead, DWG introduced Shepherd Cox as the developer.

Investors were therefore surprised and confused when Hotel Options (Lymm) Ltd was listed as the vendor on the sale and purchase agreement. "We asked DWG who Hotel Options was, and we were told that it is a company linked to Shepherd Cox that had been set up to operate the hotel," Nick said. Taking the agent's word for it, he signed the agreement and paid the remaining £92,500. Alarm bells didn't start to ring then because he began receiving the promised monthly rental return of 9% (£708) over the next few months.

Another Singaporean investor, Mr Goh, had also purchased a room at the Lymm hotel. He remembers the exact date that he received his first rental payment as it was on his wife's birthday, Oct 2, 2014. At the end of the same month, he received the second payment, which was due for November. "I thought it was such a good investment, and that my hotel room was doing very well," said the 52-year-old Goh. "I didn't suspect anything." Instead, he had imagined that he and his two sons, aged 21 and 19, could visit London on a father-son bonding trip and drive to Manchester and Liverpool to watch football matches. Goh figured that even if things went bad, he would still be the owner of a hotel room, even if it was a budget hotel on the M6 motorway near Manchester.

Goh remembers receiving his monthly payments for December and January. But there was no payment in February. In March, as no payment was forthcoming, he called DWG who simply referred him to their legal department, "which is basically just one person, Anil Dube [the legal counsel of DWG]", recalls Goh.

However, before he could contact Dube he received an email from the UK legal practitioners specialising in corporate recovery and insolvency, Begbies Traynor, informing him that Hotel Options (Lymm) had been put into administration. "When things like that happen, there's nothing much you can do, but sit down and weigh your options," he said philosophically.

It was only upon perusing the administrator's statement of proposals filed by Begbies Traynor that the investors of Ibis Lymm learnt what transpired before they came into the picture. Hotel Options (Lymm) was set up on June 6, 2013, by four shareholders in the UK, each holding 25 shares in the company worth £1 each. The same shareholders had also set up another company, Hotel Options (Knutsford), on June 5, 2013.

The shareholders of both companies purchased two existing hotel buildings and proceeded to refurbish them with the help of

Warwickshire Construction Ltd, the same firm of contractors introduced to us by The Twins to undertake work at the Lancaster hotel. Hotel Options then acquired a franchise from Accor Group to run the properties as Ibis Budget Knutsford and Ibis Budget Warrington Lymm Services, according to a press release by Accor in April 2014.

The shareholders of Hotel Options (Lymm) and Hotel Options (Knutsford) engaged Shepherd Cox as the marketing agent to sell the individual rooms of both hotel properties to investors in Singapore and the Far East. They would then be leased back to the hotel management company, which would manage the properties and generate an investment return for the individual hotel room investors, according to the administrator's report.

Shepherd Cox was to receive a commission for the sale of the rooms, and upon achieving a certain sales target within a specified time period, it would have the right to purchase the Ibis hotel at Knutsford, according to legal practitioners Marshall Peters, the administrator for Hotel Options (Knutsford). For the property at Lymm, if Shepherd Cox achieved a certain level of sales within a specific time frame, the hotel would be transferred to an associate company of Shepherd Cox called SCX Lymm Ltd that was set up for that purpose.

However, sometime in November 2014, a dispute arose between Shepherd Cox and the shareholders of Hotel Options (Knutsford) and (Lymm), mainly over the payment of commissions and whether the minimum sales target had been achieved within the stipulated time frame, according to the administrator's report. Consequently, Shepherd Cox took legal action against both Hotel Options (Knutsford) and (Lymm).

At Ibis Budget Knutsford, of a total 32 rooms, 30 were purchased by investors in Singapore and two by UK investors. The price they paid per room was £82,500 and the same 8% rental yield was promised, with annual gross rental of £6,600 and monthly rental of £550, according to the administrator's statement of proposals.

When Hotel Options (Knutsford) was unable to pay its debts, a decision was taken to appoint an administrator and a notice of its intention to do so was filed in court on Jan 22. Clive Morris of Marshall Peters Ltd was appointed the administrator of the company on Feb 5.

According to Marshall Peters' report in March, while Hotel Ibis Knutsford was viable as a going concern, it was unable to generate enough revenue to cover the monthly rental payments due to the investors. The administrator therefore approached the investors to consent to a waiver of their rental payments during the administration period.

Subsequently, when Hotel Options (Lymm) was put into administration in March, the same request was made to investors to waive their entitled rent during the eight-week administration period. The Ibis Budget Lymm has 61 rooms, of which 29 were purchased by 21 investors from Singapore and

32 by those from Taiwan. Most of the investors in Singapore had agreed to the waiver.

In keeping with the Ibis Knutsford, while the Lymm property could generate a "tiny profit" and break even operationally, this was insufficient to meet the promised rental returns due to the individual investors based on the 8% rental yield, which would translate into about £40,000 a month ,"which would render profitable trade impossible", according to the administrators. According to an investor who would only be identified as Mr Tan, the investors were told that they could buy the freehold title if they wanted to. Tan and his wife were the biggest investors of the two Ibis budget hotels, having purchased two rooms at Knutsford and four at Lymm for a total of over $1 million.

Tan, along with the other Singaporean investors at Ibis Knutsford, was keen to purchase the freehold title of the property. Buying the freehold title meant that they could appoint their own hotel management company. They were even willing to negotiate with Accor Group to have the contract renewed so the hotel could continue operating under the Ibis Budget brand.

Tan was eventually told that the freehold title for the Ibis Knutsford would cost £20,000, while the same title for the hotel at Lymm was about £40,000. The Singaporean investors therefore submitted a bid of £21,000 for the freehold title of the Knutsford property. "We thought we would get the freehold title, but at the eleventh hour, we were told by the administrator that Shepherd Cox has the freehold title for Knutsford and has since taken hold of the freehold title for Lymm as well". The investors, meanwhile, own a 978-year leasehold title on the individual hotel rooms.

The investors of Ibis Lymm in Singapore also learnt that Taiwanese investors in the same property appeared to have got a better deal, thanks to their agent. The investors in Taiwan had continued to receive their 8% return, as Shepherd Cox and the "intermediary in Taiwan" had deposited £60,000 "to cover potential rental costs", according to the administrator's report. In the final progress report, another £20,000 was deposited with the instructed solicitors by the Taiwan intermediary. "The Taiwanese creditors had difficulty providing the waiver due to translation issues, and the fact that there are no analogous proceedings to an administration in Taiwan," said administrator Begbies Traynor in its final progress report on July 3.

The Taiwan intermediary, Joe Yang, CEO of Soufun Taiwan, said as none of the investors in Taiwan spoke English, he had to represent them. Yang had marketed the Ibis Lymm hotel to the investors in Taiwan, and his firm is said to be the leading firm when it comes to marketing overseas property. Soufun has been able to continue paying the investors in Taiwan, as the company had taken out a £100,000 insurance policy to protect its investors in case problems arose with the transactions, explains Yang. He also negotiated with Shepherd

Cox to keep the same rental guarantee of 8% for his Taiwanese investors.

Unfortunately, they had simply paid too much. When asked how they arrived at the price of £94,500, Lee Bramzell said they calculated it based on the projected room rates multiplied by the number of days and the number of years and used a present value model to arrive at the price of the room.

Shepherd Cox was now on its way to bigger things and building that portfolio of fifteen or twenty hotels. To achieve that however, they would need help. Financial help. For some of that they turned to Stuart Davies and his lending business, A Shade Greener Finance Ltd (ASG).

ASG lent to Shepherd Cox on at least four separate properties in Manchester, Halifax, Chester, and Bicester. All four loans were eventually repaid fully to ASG, no doubt to the considerable relief of Stuart Davies. Though on two occasions it appears that further borrowing was taken out in order to repay ASG. These new loans came from Luqa Ltd which appears not to be a traditional lender but probably private investors who, according to Companies House appear to be a man and wife now in their late seventies. It is to be hoped they didn't lose their pensions as a result of the failure of Shepherd Cox.

Other banks were not quite so fortunate. Aldermore Bank PLC have outstanding loans to SC along with Bridging Finance Ltd, one of the Henry Moser's, Together group of companies, who I also tried to warn of the dangers of UCIS schemes. Lenders into UCIS schemes also include:

- Fiduciam
- Mysing Capital
- Assetz Capital
- Hope Capital
- Lloyds Bank
- Allied Irish Bank
- NatWest
- Northern Rock

It is highly likely there are others to add to this list. You may well be wondering what their compliance teams were doing when loans were made or when releases were granted to enable investors leases to be registered at the Land Registry. Furthermore, if a bank was requested to lend on these schemes but declined because their compliance team was awake, they also had a duty to report their suspicions in the form of a Suspicious Activity Report (SAR). If potential money laundering or other violations are detected, a report is required. Suspicious activity can refer to any individual, incident, event, or activity that seems unusual or out of place. We need to remember that establishing, operating, or managing an unregulated collective investment scheme is a criminal offence. Once potential criminal activity is detected, the SAR must be filed within 30 days.

One of the earliest hotel schemes to fail was The Corran. Back in 2015, the future seemed bright and promising for Corran Resort & Spa. The hotel had just relaunched as a luxury property and had invited Welsh celebrities to partake in a spa experience in their six new treatment rooms. However, it slowly became apparent that all was not as it seemed behind the scenes. Throughout 2017 and 2018, the hotel regularly closed and re-opened due to mismanagement, confusing locals and tourists alike.

In the meantime, more than £19 million was raised from hundreds of investors around the world. Their money should have been used to fund extensive plans to build more than 200 lodges on the Laugharne property, but the plans were rejected by the Carmarthenshire Council planners.

The Corran's troubled history includes selling shares in rooms to investors, who lost around £17 million. Sales of interests in rooms and fractions of rooms began in 2012, before the hotel reopened in 2013 after closure in a previous period of administration. The new owner was Kayboo Ltd, and sister company East Marsh Operational Company Ltd managed the business. Both went into administration on October 18th, 2016, the date on which the administrator, then HBG Corporate Ltd of Tarleton, Preston, approved a deal by which a company called Glendore Real Estate Ltd bought the hotel for £150,000.

The sequence of brief ownerships and associated management continued with Glendore Real Estate Ltd, and Plustocks Management Ltd. Two former directors of these companies, County West Secretarial Services Ltd and Mr Keith Stiles, were also directors of Kayboo, which is now in the hands of liquidators Wilson Field, based in Sheffield.

It seems uncertain whether any monies will be recovered. Kayboo Ltd, and its sister company East Marsh Operational Co Ltd, should have stopped trading in 2015, when it was clear that the business was in trouble, but the directors accepted investments of a further £500,000. Large payments were made to third parties, both connected and unconnected, without evidence of work done or services rendered, but given the bankruptcies of a number of these third parties, those payments appear to have disappeared beyond the reach of creditors. The liquidators are dealing with 278 claims from unsecured creditors, totalling £14.429 million. In addition, a further 151 creditors, owed £3.155 million, have not submitted claims. It has also been reported that one of Kayboo's two directors had died of Covid-19.

One of the biggest and perhaps most flamboyant failures is that of the Carlauren Group where investors were fleeced of upwards of £75m, largely in to care homes.

Carlauren founder Sean Murray appears to have had a taste for the high life, literally, spending what look like company funds on supercars, a yacht, and a private jet in which he is said to have flown around the world. He is described as a man with "a limp handshake and an obsession with designer clothes", who boasted of being married seven times and has been dubbed a "Walter Mitty" character. Administrators say he bought the luxury vehicles through a company called Carlauren Travel and claimed they were for the purpose of servicing the company's rich clientele.

Joint administrators Quantuma told investors it had obtained a £40 million freezing order over Murray's assets in the High Court in London. However, neither Quantuma nor Duff & Phelps can estimate how much money will be returned to investors, due in part to the state of record keeping at Carlauren.

In another statement, Quantuma and Duff & Phelps revealed they have seized the cars (thought to include a Rolls-Royce, a Bentley, a Ferrari, and a Lamborghini), the yacht and the jet with a view to selling them. Two luxury homes allegedly lived in by Murray and his latest wife are expected to go the same way.

Murray, however, was not the only man with an interesting past at Carlauren. Paul Murphy, Carlauren's "executive consultant, investor sales" allegedly has "over 20 years' experience in UK and international real estate". Some of it appears to have been spent in jail as he was sentenced to six years in 2011 for his part in a boiler-room scam.

Murphy was not the only sales outlet Carlauren used. Other agents such as One Touch Solutions, also sold units for the company and got 15% commission. Investors have questioned why they were paid so well when most property agents charge 1%-2%.

A battle is now afoot between Carlauren investors and the Financial Conduct Authority with investors hoping for compensation. A response from the FCA is interesting, "Carlauren was not authorised by the FCA. On the basis of the evidence, we have seen it does not appear to have been a collective investment scheme, but we will, of course, consider any further evidence that may come to light.". As the Carlauren scheme has been known about for some considerable time a number of lawyers have already looked at its structure. UAP have received scheme documents from a number of Carlauren clients. Needless to say, it looks a lot like a duck!

Whilst we have looked at developments that have failed it`s just as important to be aware of those that are still being marketed to the general public. I receive at least one new sales promotion of a new scheme every week. The vast majority are clearly UCIS and the rest are borderline. By that I mean, for example, whether the purchase of a lodge to be let out within a holiday complex is a collective? It`s certainly one of many looked after by a centralised manager and the deal offers a guaranteed return which suggests pooling. It`s necessary to remember that a collective investment scheme can be in "anything", according to the Bank of England. It requires only that the participants do not have day-to-day control and either have pooled income or be managed as a whole. Where there is a single, centralised "manager" of the property and/or guaranteed returns the requirements will be fulfilled unless the developer has stumped up and deposited sufficient cash to cover all returns throughout the period of the scheme. That`s nigh on impossible.

At 9.15am on Wednesday the 27th of April 2022 I was contacted by Farrbury Capital Partners with details of a new hotel investment opportunity. This is the email I received:

Dear Neil,

Thank you for your enquiry in to the newly launched, 4-star, Radisson Hotel investment.

Please see below the latest investment brochure and due diligence brochure.

Brochure –

https://www.farrbury.com/Brochure/Farrbury_Radisson_E
bbsfleet_InvestmentBrochure.pdf

Due Diligence –

https://www.farrbury.com/Brochure/Farrbury_Radisson_E
bbsfleet_DDReport.pdf

The Radisson at Ebbsfleet is a 55 room, 4-star hotel, operated and managed by the Radisson Group. Its prime location makes it the perfect stopover for the nearly 60 million, leisure and business tourists who visit the area each year. Located only 17 minutes from Central London and 2 hours from both Paris and Brussels, it offers investors an unrivalled play into the London hotel investment market.

The investment offers interest on funds during the build, followed by 10 years of guaranteed returns and a guaranteed buyback between years 5 and 10 at 150% of the purchase price. This represents an annualised net yield of 14%.

Key Investment Highlights

- Invest from £225,000+VAT
- 998-year leasehold
- 10-year guaranteed return
- Buyback between years 5-10 at 150% of purchase price
- Completion – July 2024
- Outstanding accessibility
- Pay in installments
- Planning Permission Granted

Please let me know if you have any questions.

Kind regards,

James

James Hayward

Director, Farrbury Capital Partners

Since receiving the original email from Farrbury Capital I have asked them a number of questions. This is the email track which has passed between us:

From: Neil Bromage <neil@neilbromage.com>
Sent: Sunday, June 5, 2022 1:33 PM
To: James Hayward <james@farrbury.com>
Subject: RE: Radisson Hotel investment

James,

I`d be grateful if you would confirm:

1. Who is responsible for making payment of the 7-10% returns?

2. On what basis is the return guaranteed?

3. On what <u>contractual</u> basis will the management company operate the rooms?

4. When will construction begin?

Thanks. **Kind regards,**

Neil

From: James Hayward <james@farrbury.com>
Sent: 06 June 2022 12:23
To: Neil Bromage <neil@neilbromage.com>
Subject: RE: Radisson Hotel investment

Hi Neil,

Thank you for your email, please see the answers below.

1. Who is responsible for making payment of the 7-10% returns?

The SPV, Ebbsfleet Hotel 1 Ltd will be responsible for paying all returns, which will be passed on by Radisson from the generated income. All investors will also have an equal share in Ebbsfleet Hotel Security Ltd, which holds a £5.5 million charge over the land and asset, ensuring all funds are asset backed.

2. On what basis is the return guaranteed?

I have provided the wording for you in the contract regarding the returns.

Guaranteed Income

In the event that in any one Service Charge Year following the date of this lease until a date which is ten years from the date of this lease or (if later) the expiration of the tenth Service Charge Year following the date of this lease the Tenants Distribute Income for said year is less than the Forecasted Income for such year, the Landlord shall pay to the

Tenant the difference between two such incomes.

Forecasted Income:

> Year 1: 6.7% of the Premium
>
> Year 2: 7% of the Premium
>
> Year 3: 7.5% of the Premium
>
> Year 4: 8% of the Premium
>
> Year 5: 8.25% of the Premium
>
> Year 6: 8.5% of the Premium
>
> Year 8: 9% of the Premium
>
> Year 9: 9.25% of the Premium
>
> Year 10: 9.5% of the Premium

3. On what <u>contractual</u> basis will the management company operate the rooms?

Please see attached a legal undertaking, confirming the terms under which Radisson will operate the hotel under their 20-year operational agreement.

4. When will construction begin?

Construction will begin in a month or two, with completion set for July 2024.

I do hope this is helpful.

Kind regards,

James

James,

1. Your attached letter does not amount to a "legal undertaking" or anything remotely resembling such!

2. Ebbsfleet Hotel 1 Ltd is a shell company established in April of this year with just £100! This provides absolutely NO security that returns can be met. Additionally, as the money is going from, allegedly Radisson into Ebbsfleet No 1 Ltd there is clear and defined "pooling" of income.

With that in mind please explain:

3. Precisely why you believe this is NOT an Unregulated Collective Investment Scheme?

4. Why Radisson Hotel Group say, today, "We were not aware of this scheme nor of any involvement with it"?

Kind regards,

Neil

At the point of going to press on June 27th I've still not received a response to my email and have therefore reported the matter to the FCA.

We have already acknowledged that if something looks like a duck and quacks like a duck it probably is a duck. That being so, this is a duck, otherwise known as a Collective Investment Scheme. Page 7 of the very impressive and glossy brochure clearly states "Fully managed" and "assured rental". It's also off plan!

Another likely "duck" is the NATEX development in Liverpool. Despite receiving £12m loan to complete the 574-unit student accommodation its developers Mount Group have gone into administration owing £39m to creditors. All of the 574 units were sold off-plan to investors, some of whom have succeeded in registering unilateral notices at the Land Registry to protect their interests. According to administrators, Mazars, "The company's financial position has been adversely affected by delays and increased costs resulting from, among other factors, the Covid-19 pandemic and supply chain issues associated with the pandemic and Brexit."

All of the developers of these failed schemes appear to offer a reason for their failure, however limp it may be. Perhaps one of the best is, "Sorry, I was arrested".

That's the claim of the infamous Elliot Lawless. The Elliot Group schemes Infinity Waters, Aura and

Residence schemes are all now in administration along with the company's Epic Hotel scheme in the Baltic Quarter.

Mr Lawless, from Liverpool, was arrested on suspicion of conspiracy to defraud, bribery and corruption. He denies any wrongdoing and has consistently argued that it was his arrest and the negative publicity that undermined confidence in the schemes he was developing.

A number of investors in the scheme have now spoken about their ordeal, and how the collapse of the Infinity Waters scheme had affected their lives.

Jacqui Parker said, *"I am one of the people that thought they had bought a dream home in Liverpool. I am the mum of a teenager who is vulnerable due to a mild learning disability. As a mum but also a social worker I have always worried about my son's future and the quality of life he may have to look forward to. I always wondered what I could do to help him have the life and independence he deserves. I wanted a one bed flat for me and I wanted my son to have his own flat too so he could have some independence.....It was hard to scrape together the deposit for one flat, all my savings and some bank loans enabled me to do this. Two sets of deposit would be out of the question. Luckily enough, my friend planned to rent hers and would give me first refusal on renting it directly from her for my son. Our dream was going to become a reality……From a state of extreme happiness and contentment, knowing I could keep an eye on my lad but letting him have the independence to flourish, I have gone to a state of complete devastation……I don't know what we are going to do. I can't sleep, my concentration is shot to pieces and my son is constantly seeking reassurances from me, I just can't give. I am not sure that I will ever recover from the financial impact this has on my life. My son and I are both at sea, waiting for the ocean to swallow us up……Taking these flats from us is not just about the devastating financial impact but the dead ending of people's lives."*

Sabrina is based in France and told of her father's loss of the use of his legs after a road accident in his native Cameroon and how as a teenager, she grew up visiting her dad in hospital realising that he might not walk again. However, through pure will power her father managed to walk again but was still reliant on a wheelchair. A few years ago, he agreed to help Sabrina buy an apartment in the UK. She said: *"I chose a one-bedroom flat in Infinity Waters in Liverpool. Great development, attractive price when bought off plan, the developer had already delivered thousands of units in Liverpool, the sales agents had five stars reviews, they recommended a solicitor to assist me in the process, answered all my questions and even offered me £5000 worth of furniture……All I had to do was to deposit half now and half upon completion. It would allow me to get a mortgage, thus increasing my standards of living. The deposit was going to be held in the lawyer's Escrow account and I would accrue interests. The apartments were selling fast and after making the trip to Liverpool to check things out for myself, I went for it.....I received a phone call from my sales agent in January 2020 who told me the development was put into voluntary administration. From the sound of it, it was due to lack of funding. It was explained that, by entering administration voluntarily, the developer Elliot Lawless would be able to choose the administrator to resolve the matter favourably. The administrators in question were DRP (David Rubin and Partners who are now part of Begbies Traynor Group)."*

Sabrina joined an alliance of investors in the Infinity Waters scheme and heard yet more distressing stories. "I connected with hundreds of people from over 40 countries. The stories were heart breaking." She said she now feels a strong sense of shame. "My only hope now is that I can use the crumbs I'm left with so my father can watch me have a better life. No words can describe the shame that I feel. The guilt is unbearable.....The word "Liverpool" triggers PSTD-like symptoms. The money is gone. No consolation, just shame."

Nader lives in Bahrain. He said: "My wife and I had been putting aside some money for some time now and waiting for any opportunity that would feel right for an investment overseas. "While browsing online, we came across eye catching developments in Liverpool, and since we enjoyed coming to the UK, and seeing how property in London was too expensive, we decided to travel to Liverpool and have a look first hand at how the city has been moving forward from 10 years ago. We immediately fell in love with the city and were taken on a tour off the developments that Mr Elliott Lawless had already built."

When Elliot's schemes collapsed into administration in April 2020 David Rubin and Partners (DRP) were appointed as administrators. DRP has since merged with Begbies Traynor. The High Court has now ruled that Begbies Traynor must sell the Infinity Waters site to Infinity Development Propco Ltd (IDPL), a company which represents investors in the scheme who said that they intended to work to remove a charge on the site held by the Equity Group Limited, a Seychelles based company controlled by Mr Lawless.

In February 2022 IDPL legal team were successful at a hearing in the High Court, before his Honour Judge Mark Cawson QC, in obtaining an order for the Infinity Developments site to be sold to Infinity Development Propco Ltd (IDPL). The order allowed for the Infinity Development Site to be sold to IDPL free from the legal charge granted to and held by the second respondent in those proceedings, Virtuoso Investments Limited. The site is to be sold with the following in place: (1) the legal charge granted to and held by Equity Group Limited ('the EGL Charge'), (2) the lease granted to Infinity Developments Holdings Limited, ('the Holdings Lease'). Crucially, however, the terms of the sale also transfer the rights to challenge the EGL Charge and the Holdings Lease to IDPL. The Judge held that selling the site to IDPL on the terms of its bid represented a better outcome and therefore better return to creditors. The Judge also ordered that the three investor/purchasers who effectively represented the interests of the wider group would be entitled to recover most of their costs incurred in relation to the proceedings.

In a rather aloof statement Elliot Lawless said: "This is the third Elliot project to have been acquired by an investor consortium and it demonstrates once again that my projects benefited from prime locations and that their viability was and remains extremely strong.

It seems there is a clear identifying characteristic amongst all these developers which may be better explored in the following chapter.

SFO list of Alpha companies and schemes under investigation

1. Alpha Holdings (GB) Limited

2. Alpha Properties (Leicester) Limited

3. Alpha Developments (Leicester) Limited

4. Alpha Developments (Preston) Limited

5. Alpha Developments (Stoke1) Limited

6. Alpha Developments (Bradford) Limited

7. Alpha Developments (Loughborough) Limited

8. Alpha Developments (Bradford2) Limited

9. Alpha Developments (Stoke) Limited

10. A1 Alpha Properties (Leicester) Limited

11. Alpha Student Management Limited

12. A1 Properties (Sunderland) Limited

13. Alpha Homes Leicester Limited

14. Alpha Projects (UK) Limited

15. Alpha Developments (Huddersfield) Limited

16. Alpha Developments (Stoke2) Limited

17. AGP Holdings Limited

18. Green Parks Finance Limited

19. Green Parks (Westward Ho!) Limited

20. Westbeach Invest Limited

21. Studyrooms Direct LLP

22. Westbeach Resort Limited

23. Green Parks (Holdings) Limited

24. Green Parks Holidays Limited

25. Green Parks Holdings (Ilfracombe) Limited

26. Green Parks Holidays (Ilfracombe) Limited

Schemes:

1. Westbeach Holiday Park

2. 24-26 Norfolk Street

3. Park Lane House

4. Tudor Studios

5. College Street Village

6. The Foundry (Phases I and II)

7. Jubilee Court

8. Mandale Terrace

9. Q Studios

10. Scholars Village

11. Millfield House

12. The Box, Prestone

13. The Chapel, Ambleside

14. Scholars Court

15. Ilfracombe Holiday Village

16. Primrose Hill

17. Pre-tenanted (Hylton Road, Roker Avenue, Villette Road, Sunderland)

CHAPTER 9

Psychopaths and Ponzi`s

Charles Ponzi may well have coined the phrase and Bernie
Madoff may be its most high-profile exponent, but the first
"Ponzi" scheme appears to have been carried out by Adele
Spitzeder in 1869 – 1872.

Adelheid Luise Spitzeder was born in Berlin in 1832 and
became an actress, gaining great acclaim on her debut in 1856.
However, she was unable to achieve a level of success
sufficient to sustain her lifestyle. In 1869, in need of cash, she
borrowed approximately £400 – in today`s money, from
someone she met in Munich, promising that she knew someone
who was willing to take the sum and pay 10% a month for it.
Being an obvious opportunist, Spitzeder advertised similar
services in a newspaper and the number of people who would
lend to her increased significantly. In 1869 she set up the
Spitzedersche Privatbank. By 1872 the bank was so successful
that she was considered to be the wealthiest woman in Bavaria.

The Spitzedersche Privatbank operated as a classic Ponzi
scheme, using new deposits to pay interest to the original
depositors. Spitzeder's public philanthropy lifted the bank`s

profile and improved its reputation. She also bribed newspaper editors to defend her from accusations of fraud.

As early as 1871 reporters and officials were asking questions. But since Spitzeder wasn't breaking any laws at the time, they could do nothing, and the attacks only succeeded in attracting customers. By 1872, however, the authorities insisted she start following proper accounting procedures. Shortly afterwards, 60 customers (at the prompting of her rivals) arrived at her house and demanded their money back, causing her to flee. She was soon arrested, and the doors of the bank were closed. In 1873 Spitzeder was sentenced to nearly four years in prison. Overall, 32,000 people lost a total of £152m.

If she was the first, she most certainly will not be the last. There is indeed a long list of them, and they all appear to have something in common. They all have psychopathic tendencies. The term "psychopath" is used to describe someone who is callous, unemotional, and morally depraved, though it doesn't refer to an official diagnosis but is often used in clinical and legal settings.

Many of the characteristics of a psychopath overlap with symptoms of antisocial personality disorder, a broader mental health condition that is used to describe people who frequently break rules. But not all those with antisocial personality disorders are considered to be psychopaths. Psychopathic behaviour varies greatly from one individual to another. Some are sex offenders and murderers. But others may be successful leaders.

Psychopathic traits may emerge during childhood and grow worse over time. These are some of the most common signs of a psychopath:

Superficial Charm

Psychopaths are often likable on the surface. They're usually good conversationalists, and they share stories that make them look good. They may be funny and charismatic as well.

Need for Stimulation

Psychopaths love excitement. They like to have constant action in their lives, and they frequently want to live in the "fast lane."

Quite often, their need for stimulation involves breaking rules. They may enjoy the thrill of getting away with something, or they might even like the fact that they could "get caught" at any moment. Consequently, they often struggle to stay engaged in dull or repetitive tasks, and they may be intolerant of routines.

Pathological Lying

Psychopaths tell lies to look good and get out of trouble. But they also tell lies to cover up their previous lies. They have difficulty keeping their stories straight sometimes as they forget what they've said. If challenged by anyone, they simply change their story again or rework the facts to fit the situation.

Grandiose Sense of Self-Worth

Psychopaths have an inflated view of themselves, they see themselves as important and entitled. They often feel justified to live according to their own rules, and they think that the laws don't apply to them.

Manipulative

Psychopaths are really good at getting other people to do what they want. They may play on a person's guilt while lying to get someone else to do their work for them.

Lack of Remorse

Psychopaths don't care how their behaviour affects other people. They may forget about something that hurts someone, or they may insist that others are overreacting when their feelings are hurt. Ultimately, they don't experience any guilt for causing people pain. In fact, they often rationalize their behaviour and blame other people.

Shallow Affect

Psychopaths don't show many emotions, at least not genuine ones. They may appear cold and unemotional much of the time. But when it serves them well, they might exhibit a dramatic display of feelings. These are usually short-lived and quite shallow.

For example, they may show anger if they can intimidate someone, or they might show sadness to manipulate someone. But they don't really experience these emotions.

Lack of Empathy

Psychopaths struggle to understand how someone else might feel afraid, sad, or anxious. It just doesn't make sense to them as they're not able to read people. They're completely indifferent to people who are suffering, even when it's a close friend or family member.

Parasitic Lifestyle

Psychopaths may have sob stories about why they can't earn money, or they might often report being victimized by others. Then, they take advantage of the kindness of others by depending on them financially. They use people to get whatever they can with no regard for how a person may feel.

Poor Behavioural Controls

Psychopaths struggle to follow rules, laws, and policies much of the time. Even if they set out to follow the rules, they usually don't stick to them for long.

Promiscuous Sexual Behaviour

Since they don't care about the people around them, psychopaths are likely to cheat on their partners. They may engage in unprotected sex with strangers. Or they may use sex as a way to get what they want. Sex is not an emotional or loving act for them.

Early Behavioural Problems

Most psychopaths exhibit behavioural problems at an early age. They may cheat, skip school, vandalize property, misuse substances, or become violent. Their misbehaviours tend to escalate over time and are more serious than their peer's misbehaviours.

Lack of Realistic, Long-Term Goals

A psychopath's goal might be to become rich or be famous. But quite often, they have little idea about how to make these things happen. Instead, they insist that somehow, they'll get what they want without putting in the effort to get there.

Impulsivity

Psychopaths respond to things according to the way they feel. They don't spend time thinking about the potential risks and benefits of their choices. Instead, they want immediate gratification. So, they may quit a job, end a relationship, move to a new city, or buy a new car on a whim.

Irresponsibility

Promises don't mean anything to psychopaths. Whether they promise to repay a loan or sign a contract, they aren't trustworthy. They may shrug off child support payments, get deeply in debt, or forget about obligations and commitments.

Psychopaths don't accept responsibility for the problems in their lives. They see their issues as always being someone else's fault. They frequently play the role of the victim and enjoy sharing stories about how others have taken advantage of them.

Many Marital Relationships

Psychopaths may get married because it serves them well. For example, they may want to spend a partner's income or share their debt with someone else. But their behaviour often leads to frequent divorces as their partners eventually see them in a more accurate light.

Criminal Versatility

Psychopaths tend to view rules as suggestions—and they usually view laws as restrictions that hold them back. Their criminal behaviours can be quite varied. Driving infractions, financial violations, and acts of violence are just a few examples of the array of crimes one might commit. Of course, not all of them get incarcerated. Some may operate under shady businesses or engage in unethical practices that don't lead to an arrest.

Revocation of Conditional Release

Most psychopaths don't adhere to the rules of conditional release when they are released from prison. They may think they won't get caught again. Or they may find ways to excuse their behaviour. They might even blame "getting caught" on other people.

Whilst some aspects may be different most exponents of Ponzi schemes and other frauds have common personality traits. Carrying out significant crimes with no conscience or thought for their unsuspecting victims means that many are likely to be sociopaths or psychopaths. How else could they commit crimes of such magnitude.

Psychopaths tend to be more manipulative, can be seen by others as more charming, lead a semblance of a normal life, and minimize risk in criminal activities. Sociopaths tend to be more erratic, rage-prone, and unable to lead as much of a normal life

Much of what we have already witnessed here suggests that some of these schemers will connive and steal from the elderly and unsuspecting without an ounce of remorse.

Bernie Madoff showed absolutely no remorse after committing the largest Ponzi fraud in history. He defrauded investors out of $65 billion with a promised return of 10% per annum and was later sentenced to 150 years in prison.

But why did he do it?

As the former chairman of NASDAQ, (National Association of Securities Dealers Automated Quotations), an American stock market that handles electronic securities trading around the world Madoff was already super-rich. He was a billionaire, clearly didn`t need the money and he had all the trappings of wealth. Despite his wealth he continued to ingratiate himself with important people and move in all the right circles and was so well regarded that seasoned hedge fund managers almost worshipped him and begged to invest with him.

Talk to anyone who has been to prison and they will tell you that no-one is guilty in jail. Denial and a failure to accept responsibility apparently runs riot in those places. Madoff, even after admitting his guilt still showed a complete lack of empathy for his victims and appeared more concerned about his reputation than the ruin he had inflicted on them. But then many fraudsters are overly concerned about their image, boasting about their connections in order to feel important.

It seems then, that a grandiose, self-important attitude may lie at the heart of many conmen and the schemes they ignite. But we need to remember that not all psychopaths are perpetrators of financial fraud and not all unregulated collective investment schemes are Ponzi`s.

According to Investopedia a Ponzi scheme is a fraudulent investment scam promising high rates of return with little risk to investors. It is a fraudulent scam which generates returns for earlier investors with money taken from later investors. This is similar to a pyramid scheme in that both are based on using new investors' funds to pay the earlier backers and both eventually bottom out when the flood of new investors dries up and there isn't enough money to go around. At that point, the schemes unravel.

Put simply it`s all about robbing Peter to pay Paul.

Investopedia goes on to say that a Ponzi scheme is an investment fraud in which clients are promised a large profit at little to no risk. Companies that engage in a Ponzi scheme

212

focus all of their energy into attracting new clients to make investments. This new income is used to pay original investors their returns, marked as a profit from a legitimate transaction. Ponzi schemes rely on a constant flow of new investments to continue to provide returns to older investors. When this flow runs out, the scheme falls apart.

How then, does this fit with UCIS property scams? There will undoubtedly be some considerable debate about this question if the prosecuting authorities have an appetite for it. So, what are the similarities.

UCIS investors were all promised high rates of return without risk with the security of property minimising the latter. It seems clear that developers needed to continually sell more and more units to keep things afloat. We also know that in most if not all cases, intercompany loans were predominate and suggest that monies were being moved around at will.

It may then appear that these UCIS schemes are also Ponzi schemes. However, there is a further element to a traditional Ponzi in that the scheme leads victims to believe that profits are coming from legitimate (but non-existent) business activity, and they remain unaware that other investors are the source of funds. A Ponzi scheme can maintain the illusion of a sustainable business as long as new investors contribute new funds, and as long as most of the investors do not demand full repayment.

Whether or not any of these UCIS schemes are deemed to be Ponzi`s remains to be seen, but if such a diagnosis is put forward then the current level of likely offence categories will undoubtedly intensify.

CHAPTER 10

Anatomy of a Seagull

A summer rarely goes by without one or more television news channels reporting of seagulls swooping violently down to steal food from someone and warning us all to beware!

There`s a little devilment in all of us. The sight of a seagull swooping down at speed to steal someone`s lunch as they sit quietly on a bench or sea wall soaking up the very rare British summer sunshine can at first seem amusing. It`s only when you recognise that the bird hasn`t stolen merely a few chips but the whole meal and traumatised a holidaymaker in the process that reality and shock set in.

Welcome to the world of the investor versus the administrators where the scenario is much too similar.

As an investor you`ve handed over the cash, probably something approaching £100K, and you`ve completed the purchase of your hotel room, student pod, storage unit or room in a care home. It`s time to sit back and enjoy the returns coming in each month so that you can have more time sitting by the beach licking ice cream or enjoying those fish and chips.

216

Just as you`re getting comfortable on that sea wall or bench, and the cushion you`ve invested in is well placed to lessen the harsh reality of what`s underneath it your mobile rings and alerts you to an incoming text message. The developer has gone bust, and the administrators have been called in. Your ice cream is now on the floor and your chips are flying through the air in the mouth of that damn seagull. Or to put it another way, the income from your room has dried up, you may never see your £100K again, and you`re about to become well-acquainted with someone in the administrator's office who cares as much about you as that seagull.

It was early in 2020 that I went to London to meet with a variety of people and firms about UCIS claims. I decided that I should also meet with a firm of administrators. By this time UCIS Advice point was already in contact with hundreds of investors in the A1 Alpha scheme and it seemed sensible to meet with the administrators now in charge of that. I should add however, that I had no great expectations of anything remotely positive coming from a meeting because of the way in which administrators operate and the constraints of their brief, amongst other things.

Administration is used when a company becomes insolvent and is put under the management of a Licensed Insolvency Practitioner. An important point to note is that the directors can appoint the administrators through a court process in order to protect the company and their position as much as possible. It can therefore appear at times that the directors and the administrators are working together. If you're a creditor you may wonder who will benefit from this arrangement. This is particularly so where Pre-Pack Administration is being used by directors to protect assets and ditch creditors whilst starting over again with a brand-new phoenix-like company.

The terms 'administration' and 'receivership' are often confused but there are significant differences. Administration is designed to protect a company from legal actions that may be taken against it during a specified period of time - usually about 8 weeks. The appointed administrator will work to establish whether or not the company has any way of satisfying its creditors and, where possible, put a plan of action together to make it happen. Receivership on the other hand, is initiated by those creditors or banks that believe the business cannot pay its debts. However, in this instance directors cannot place their own company into receivership.

When investors start to smell a rat an Insolvency Practitioner (IP) is frequently seen as the exterminator. A safe haven for their investment. A neutral pair of hands. A protector. The directors have by this time relinquished all control of the company in favour of the administrator who is now in charge and the effective legal custodian of all the company's assets. At this point, the investors breathe a sigh of relief as a neutral is now running the show. Months down the road and many investors have woken up to smell the coffee and in their eyes the IP wasn't the protector or a safe haven they thought he was, he was the wolf dressed up in Grandma's clothes.

A1 Alpha Properties (Leicester) Limited went into administration on February 21st, 2019, a year before I met with insolvency practitioners Quantuma who were appointed as administrators. Alpha subsequently moved into voluntary liquidation in February 2021 having been in administration for almost two years.

A1 Alpha Properties (Leicester) Limited was not the main development company in the Alpha scheme but merely a management company. According to investors in the scheme Quantuma appointed a creditors committee to look over their shoulders. One particular investor claims that this committee was secretive and that some members of it were not leaseholders and should not have been on the committee. Quantuma were tasked to gather information to show that the directors were involved in running a UCIS and may also have breached their fiduciary duties as directors.

With the results of those investigations to hand it seems that Quantuma chose not to offer the information to the prosecuting authorities but instead reached a compromise with the company's directors. This involved various management companies being transferred to the investors, many of whom did not want this as their developments, such as Scholars Village in Bradford were never likely to make a profit. Nevertheless, Quantuma pushed through on the deal and seemingly ignored the best interests of those investors because the Creditors Committee told them that's what everyone wanted. In reality, not everyone was consulted and there may well have been some ulterior motives in those committee members who appeared not to be leaseholders but represented the interests of "others".

I met with Mark Hendricks and Carl Jackson at Quantuma and had a perfectly pleasant meeting with them. But despite a few emails after the meeting in which they were provided with information on other potential UCIS schemes nothing transpired to further the relationship, though I'm aware that Quantuma are involved in a number of our UCIS Hit List Targets.

There are many investors who feel deeply aggrieved by the way in which administrators have managed the schemes they have invested in. Len invested £280k in two hotel rooms at the Northern Powerhouse Developments Caer Rhun Hall where eighty rooms fetched a total of £7.7m before going into administration.

In May 2020, Duff and Phelps, as administrators, received an offer of £1.9m for Caer Rhun Hall of which initially £75,000 related to the freehold. The buyer was also offering the investors and room owners 21p in the pound to surrender their leases. This offer remained on the table until August 2020 when the administrators cancelled the sale and accepted £750,000 for the freehold with nothing being offered to the leaseholders who appear to have been left out in the cold, highlighting the real problem for investors once administrators get involved.

The new freeholder of Caer Rhun Hall is Aaron Mellor of Tokyo Industries and is largely a nightclub operator, and not an insubstantial one. I met Aaron Mellor in 2014 at the behest of –

again - the Twins. Stewart Lewis and Steve Gaunt, who you'll remember from earlier. They wanted me to look at a property Mellor owned in York and which they thought would make a good hotel.

Mellor eventually acquired the freehold of Caer Rhun Hall for £700,000 having had the original sum reduced in court by £50,000 due to the deterioration of the property. It transpires that no maintenance was carried out whilst the property was empty for two years and there was no heating in the building despite Duff and Phelps recovering around £6m from NPD.

Having failed to get investors leases cancelled by a court D&P handed over the hotel to Mellor who is now asking investors to pay for refurbishment's and refusing to make any offer for the leases. It is also understood that he intends to operate the building, utilising the rooms owned by investors as something other than what they were designed for (but which doesn't affect the structure being a UCIS) – a tactic which is becoming increasingly noticed.

The real issue with this is that in enabling the sale of the hotel to a new buyer Duff and Phelps (which has now changed its name to Kroll) have merely passed on an unregulated collective investment scheme to a new owner even though, at the first meeting of creditors they acknowledged that NPD was running an unregulated scheme. Whether Aaron Mellor is or is not aware of this is largely irrelevant as it's still clearly a UCIS, which is still unlawful and operating it is still a criminal offence.

As Aaron Mellor's phone number is still stored in my mobile I called him up to talk about what's gone on. He said he is "White Knight" but failed to revert with further comment after I told him that he's running an unregulated collective investment scheme. The freehold may have been sold to him by the administrators but that doesn't change the legal structure.

Len and his wife are in their eighties and all their savings are now lost to this venture. They will struggle to see Mellor as the White Knight he claims to be. They are having to sell their own property and can no longer afford to live and pay the service charge fees. It is perhaps then, not surprising that having lost nearly £300K they feel more than a little unhappy that Duff and Phelps have submitted bills for their fees totalling c£340,000 as of October 2020. Further sums are likely to fall due for another year in administration.

If I hear one overriding comment about the role of insolvency practitioners in all these failed schemes it is that they are only interested in racking up huge fees for as long as possible. It certainly appears that nothing moves swiftly in the world of insolvency but what constraints are there to ensure that practitioners are not simply fleecing everyone involved.

The Insolvency (England and Wales) Rules 2016 set out the remuneration principles which provide that practitioners are entitled to remuneration and that it must be fixed as a percentage value of property or assets realised and/or distributed, time properly spent, or as a set amount or even a combination of the above.

Unless whatever literary powers I had have deserted me that means they can charge whatever they like. Though it should be added that there is a right of appeal to the courts.

However, barrister, Tom Carpenter-Leitch of Tanfield Chambers successfully resisted an application by Joint Administrators of Carlauren to have their fees and expenses paid from investors' assets. As Counsel he appeared in the Insolvency & Companies Court on behalf of two hundred investors resisting an application by the administrators. The application sought directions, by way of an extension to the *Berkeley Applegate* jurisdiction, permitting the payment of the administrator's fees and expenses so that they might be paid from the properties of the investors rather than the properties of the insolvent estates. In any other language this means that what's yours is mine (and even if not, I am taking it).

ICC Judge Prentis refused to grant the directions sought, or any directions.

The joint administrators, Duff and Phelps and Quantuma took control of, secured and insured the properties having received valuation advice stating that the properties might be worth some £24.75 million if sold "unencumbered" by the investor leases, but that they were essentially unsaleable with those leases in place.

781 leases had been granted to Investors, of which 687 had been properly registered at the Land Registry. The administrators unsuccessfully attempted to persuade investors to surrender their leases having already incurred fees in the region of £2.6 million and also £1.3 million in legal costs. Without any obvious way to be paid or reimbursed, the administrators applied to the court for directions that would have enabled the administrators to pay their fees and expenses, both those directly related to holding and selling the properties and also all those of the insolvencies more generally (including the litigation against Sean Murray) from the sale proceeds of the properties.

The administrators claimed that principle expounded in the *Berkeley Applegate* case might be extended to enable their fees and expenses to be paid from the sales proceeds of the Investors' leasehold interests. The administrators recognised that the investors leases, at least where registered, had vested the legal interests in the land in the investors, but by extending the *Berkeley Applegate* principle sought to require the investors interests to bear a share of the insolvency costs.

The administrators clearly recognised their argument was not going to succeed and changed their position at the hearing of the application. The application then became one simply to declare the administrator's rights over the freeholds.

The Judge concluded that the principal directions sought on the application served no purpose in a decision that closes another door to administrators of failed unitised property ownership schemes who seek to override the legal rights of leasehold investors.

In 2013 a review of Insolvency Practitioners fees was undertaken for the Insolvency Service. It began as follows:

Concerns continue to be raised regarding the charges, including both remuneration and expenses, made by insolvency practitioners (IPs) and the impact that this has on the position of unsecured creditors and personal debtors in insolvency situations. That such concerns exist is not generally disputed; nor would many claim that there have been no cases involving excessive fees. Beyond that, opinion about the extent of unreasonable, or even excessive, fees is divided. So, too, is opinion on the efficacy of the control and redress mechanisms that exist. But the evidence base is thin. A recent market study conducted by the Office of Fair Trading (OFT), however, concluded that the relatively weak bargaining power of unsecured creditors in insolvency situations can lead to detriment, although the basis for this conclusion has been disputed by the insolvency profession.

For those who are interested the report's conclusions can be found in the appendices at the end of this book.

There are, frankly, many sorry tales in this UCIS story. One of them is that too many investors have placed their trust in administrators to a level which cannot be met by the latter. I have told numerous investors on dozens of telephone calls that they simply should not expect an administrator to help them. They may not be against you but they're not fully for you either.

The unfortunate reality is that it simply isn't the administrator's job to look after the interests of leaseholders who are not creditors of the company. The administrator may well pay lip service and even invite investor representatives on to a committee to oversee what's being done but ultimately his function is to see if the company can be rescued from its dire state. Investors with leasehold interests in rooms or units do not qualify as creditors unless owed rent by the company being administrated.

This was reflected very clearly when Duff and Phelps and Quantuma resorted to court proceedings to override investors leasehold interests. It was further demonstrated when the same insolvency practitioner (D&P) sold the freehold of Caer Rhun Hall to the detriment of the investors. It is even questionable whether the administrator owes any duty of care to investors because they are not clients. Unfortunately, this probably means as leaseholders, investors have even fewer rights than the local milkman.

If there's a subject that investors are particularly vocal on it's administrators. These are just a few of the emails I've received:

Hi Neil

The FSA are incompetent idiots who come in, disrupt things and then just bugger off leaving investors high and dry- e.g., with Park First but also MBI, had they not interferred it may be we would still be getting paid

Action Fraud are a complete waste of time and NEVER investigate and never answer a call within 30 mins, but they are the only way to report such crimes.

SRA also just look after their own and refuse to pay out any compensation despite evidence of wrongdoing

Police are usless and say these are 'civil matters'

The only agency who has helped a bit have been the Insolvency Service - where Ron Popely was eventually struck off - again (the hotel fraud)

happy to discuss further,

Regards

John Francis (Brentwood)

Hi Neil,

Our view is that the Administrators are there purely to collate facts and figures and also to make a lot of serious money for themselves. They have been no support in any way for the victims. Many promises of monthly updates which are basically repeated for a few months to nothing at all 3 years on. We obtain more info from social media. Investors will be at the bottom of the link at for any financial recovery.

Property promoters such as Rightmove etc, and Facebook need more regulation to prevent more victims lives being destroyed, it's not just about the money.

Action Fraud have not taken any action apart from sending a couple of PSO,s to our house offering support, not that they could do anything about it from our view.

From: David >

Sent: 31 May 2022 09:09

To: neil@neilbromage.com

Subject: Property scam

Hi Neil, yes unfortunately I was part of the property scam . The same FA put me into Gavin Woodhouse Northern Powerhouse Developments & Sean Murray he of the Carlaurean fame who got away with everything. The real crooks are the companies appointed by the courts to liquidate the assets . They charge exhorbitant fees whilst literally "doing nothing" thereby ensuring any assets that were left get taken to pay their crazy fees.

Kind Regards, David

CHAPTER 11

The Sun Always Rises

If you've ever seen or read Victor Hugo's Les Misérables you will know that even the darkest night will end, and the sun will always rise.

I've been privileged to listen to and read many investors' stories for this book and as in every walk of life I've seen how everyone handles things very differently. I vividly recall one investor calling me two or three times, always whilst he was driving, wanting help to get his money back but being very afraid of what the developer would do to him. He had been bullied and threatened by a Liverpool developer of oriental decent to the extent he feared for his safety. There have been those who have confessed to suicidal feelings and, I'm told, at least one investor who simply did it. He took his own life.

I don't know whether that individual realised there was a solution to the problem but there is. Whilst I know that many of you reading this will by now have at least some idea of what it is, this is for those who may not know.

Whilst The FSMA provides a statutory right for investors to be compensated for their loss most people are not aware of this and even if they are, do not understand it. They are not alone. Recently, one significant law firm which is actively involved in this arena lost a claim for compensation in the High Court simply because they had failed to understand the wording of the Act.

What has to be remembered here is that Collective Investment Schemes fall within "Regulated Activities" according to the Financial Services and Markets Act and are regulated by the FCA. It is a criminal offence, contrary to *sections 19, 22*and *23* of *FSMA 2000*, in conjunction with the *Financial Services and Markets Act 2000 (Regulated Activities) Order 2001*, to run an unregulated CIS. In addition to any criminal sanction, *section 26* of *FSMA 2000* provides that any contract made in relation to such activity is unenforceable, in addition to compensation and restitution being available remedies to the participant.

FSMA 2000 s26 Agreements made by unauthorised persons.

(1)An agreement made by a person in the course of carrying on a regulated activity in contravention of the general prohibition is unenforceable against the other party.

(2)The other party is entitled to recover—

(a)any money or other property paid or transferred by him under the agreement; and (b)compensation for any loss sustained by him as a result of having parted with it.

The statute creates a clear route to recovery of losses because the agreement entered into is unlawful. However, this particular right of recovery is only against the person or organisation with which the agreement was made. In other words, the developer.

It's understandable that an investor will automatically want to sue the developer, but what's the point. That's one of the first things I've had to say to many investors I've spoken to. Their anger and frustration and that they want to take that out on the developer is clear to see, but there's very little point because the money will be gone before they get even close to recovering.

Two years ago, following receipt of Counsel's Advice on the initial test case in the A1 Alpha scheme, it was identified that the way in which investors can recover their losses is not by reliance solely on the provisions of the Financial Services and Markets Act. Whilst the legislation is in fine in theory it's unlikely to help in practice.

What then for the investor. The answer is simply professional negligence claims. The solicitor who acted on the purchase of units in these types of schemes have almost certainly neglected their client's interests because they have allowed and advised on the acquisition of an illegal product.

There is a strong argument in both contract and tort that solicitors were negligent in these matters. The arguments will be stronger where the solicitor has acted for multiple parties on identical transactions in the same property investment scheme.

Currently, claims in this arena are being settled by insurers and one law firm actively involved in this has recently achieved settlement of 80% of the amounts claimed.

There are already many group claims being pursued by solicitors on behalf of investor clients. Alpha, Northern Powerhouse Developments, Merderco, Carlauren, Shepherd Cox, and many others are already in the process of actively seeking to recover their losses by way of a professional negligence claim. But that doesn't even account for half of the 450 developments on the UAP Hit List.

However, whilst recovery of loss is very much in sight there are potential hurdles to overcome. The biggest is that of aggregation of the policy of insurance.

Most firms of solicitors involved in these schemes are small to medium in size. Each firm must comply with the Solicitors Regulation Authority Indemnity Insurance Rules which state that the amount of cover they must provide for every single claim is at least £2m and depending on the nature of the firm £3m.

If you've purchased a hotel room or student pod for example, you've probably paid out and lost around £75k and therefore the solicitor's insurance will more than cover your loss.

However, where a large group of claimants comes together the total amount of the claim could be significant (e.g., over £10 million) and if treated as one single claim as result of the aggregation clause found in all these policies the insurance may be insufficient to provide full restitution for each and every investor.

The issue of aggregation is a potentially complex one. The most recent authority on it can be found in the Supreme Court case of AIG v Woodman. The conclusion of the decision by the court in that matter was that the application of the aggregation clause is highly fact sensitive. It will depend upon the relevant matters or transactions being viewed in the round. Any earlier notion of interdependence or intrinsic relationships have now been dispensed with. The test for whether transactions are related is simply whether there is a real connection between them, or in other words, whether they fit together.

That is likely to be good news for the vast majority of claimants in these matters.

However, it may not be of equally good news for a particular class of investors, those who have purchased off plan! We know that the FCA have expressed their own concerns about off-plan developments. This could be particularly problematic if you`ve purchased what`s described as an "apartment" in a block yet to be developed.

There is currently a noticeable switch in the types of development all the investment sales companies are promoting.

Whilst most people are now alert to the scam of student accommodation and rooms in almost anything the simple apartment can appear to be without danger. If, however, the development has been structured (possibly unwittingly) as a collective investment scheme (pooled income and single management) there could well be a problem. In this instance its quite likely that all those purchases could be deemed as "related" and "fitting together" as the development is unlikely to go ahead without the investor's funds.

CHAPTER 12

Warning Signs

Death and taxes may well be the only certainties in life but there will always be conmen, charlatans and fraudsters too. Whatever the state does to legislate against certain activity there will always be someone who tries to get around it. For these reasons investors need to be sensitive to red flags, those relatively easy to detect signs that can prevent them from losing their shirt.

FCA Regulated

Whilst not all property investment is regulated it should be if it's structured as a Collective Investment Scheme. If it looks like it is then you should immediately check with the Financial Conduct Authority (FCA) at www.fca.org.uk whether or not the developer, and ideally the sales company is registered.

Structure

Ostriches! Remember that a UCIS can be anything. You should look out for the two clear indicators:

- Pooled Income – either all the sale proceeds or all the rental income.

- Pooled Management – one single rental management company looking after everything, generally appointed by the developer.

Solicitors

One of the mistakes many investors have made is not using their own solicitor. Almost all these schemes will recommend a solicitor to buyers. Those law firms churn out these sales like breeding rabbits. In many cases they have already been briefed by the developer with whom they have a relationship. Don`t ignore the fact that whenever a potential buyer uses their own solicitors most of those sales do not proceed because the independent lawyer sees through the façade and recognises the other problems.

Exclusivity

We all love to have something unique, something no-one else has or can get. When we`re offered something which is exclusive to us we are immediately attracted to it.

Many of the sales agents touting UCIS schemes use the "exclusive" tag when selling to investors. "I can only do this for you"; "You`re getting the best room in the hotel"; "This deal is exclusive for today only". These are all phrases you`ll here at some point. You need to ask yourself why this amazing opportunity is being offered only to you.

Too Good to be True

Living, as I do in a seaside town I`ve become used to
holidaymakers who forget to pack the most important ingredient
for a good holiday. Common sense. They will happily walk
across busy roads in front of oncoming vehicles, drink more
than they can handle, and wonder why the accommodation they
are staying in is grubby having paid only £15 a night for the
privilege of staying there.

Everybody knows that if something looks too good to be true
it usually is. Your common sense tells you that almost
immediately. If it has, then just ask yourself why you`re being
offered such a high rate of return with this deal when the norm
on the high street is only a fraction of that. More to the point,
why is the developer going to buy it back in five or ten years'
time. He won`t because hardly any of these developers last
more than a year or two before closing the company down.

Pack your common sense in shed loads when you`re
reviewing investment offers.

Authors Note

Whilst I've spent some considerable time writing this book I would have liked to spend more. I'm conscious that I've only really scratched the surface of this murky and almost incestuous environment. As I've said in the book there are hundreds more of these schemes out there and which are likely to fail. I'm quite sure that there will be some investors who would have liked more coverage of the scheme they found themselves in but time and space dictate that it simply wasn't possible.

The legendary Bing Crosby said in High Society that "there's a little larceny operating in all of us" and to different degrees I believe that's right. There will of course be those amongst you who are now jumping up and down, distraught with anger at that suggestion, but consider this. I once met a man who worked for the Post Office, a gentle inoffensive chap whose sister was a Dominican Nun. Within his work, and from time to time he had to go out of town, often to London and his employer paid his expenses. Rather than stay in a hotel he stayed with family but still claimed the usual expenses that everyone else claimed. I imagine there are lots of folk out there who have done a similar thing. He was sent to prison for six months for theft. Similarly, I know people who when they needed a new stair carpet "accidentally" knocked a tin of paint down the stairs and claimed on their insurance. That's fraud. I know plenty of people in business who regularly don`t account for all their income or charge customers in cash to avoid the VAT. The old crooner, as Crosby was known, was right in what he said. We are all just a little corrupt. But the reason I`ve said this is that I am grateful that the FCA wrote to us about the Lancaster hotel project. I`m equally grateful to the individual who reported the matter to the FCA – they know who they are. That intervention probably saved my life and enabled this book to be written to warn as many investors as possible about the dangers of these unregulated schemes.

Acknowledgements

Many people have helped me with this book and I`m unlikely to remember them all here. So many investors have given generously of their time and provided me with information, and I thank each and every one of them.

I have also reviewed a number of media outlets and articles for information which I have then dissected and disseminated in order to tell stories that fitted the model and parameters of this book. In particular, The Guardian, BBC, The Liverpool Echo, Manchester Evening News, Wales Online and West Wales News. I am grateful to them all.

Finally, I can`t close without thanking the most important person in my life, without whose constant encouragement and belief over nearly 47 years of marriage, I wouldn`t be writing this now. She has put up with me being locked into my study for hours and hours over many weeks and months and has never once said the grass needs cutting or when am I going to wash the dishes. Thankyou!

About The Author

Neil Bromage is an award-winning writer and journalist. Over more than twenty-five years he has written for The Times, Sunday Times, Telegraph, Daily Mail and Mail on Sunday on a range of business topics. He has also interviewed high profile business leaders for a variety of magazines. He is the author of a major report, Delivering on the ePromise: Strategies for Successful Fulfilment in the New Economy, which was commissioned and published by Reuters Business Insight. How to Books published 100 Ways to Make Your Business a Success. Neil`s first novel The Money-Go-Round was published in 2022 and is written under the pseudonym C.J. Neill.

Neil is married and lives by the sea in Blackpool, in the northwest of the UK with his wife and two standard, long-haired Dachshund`s.

You can learn more about Neil`s work at www.neilbromage.com and www.cjneill.com

APPENDICES

1. Financial Services and Markets Act 2000 s235
    Collective Investment Schemes
2. Financial Services and Markets Act 2000:
    Arrangements not amounting to a Collective
    Investment Scheme
3. Review of Insolvency Practitioners Fees
4. Bank of England / Financial Markets Law
    Committee Report: Legal assessment of problems
    associated with the definition of Collective
    Investment Scheme and related terms
5. Suella Braverman MP – Letter
6. Statutory Investor Certificates
7. A1 Alpha Worldwide Freezing Order

Financial Services and Markets Act 2000

235Collective investment schemes.

(1)In this Part "collective investment scheme" means any arrangements with respect to property of any description, including money, the purpose or effect of which is to enable persons taking part in the arrangements (whether by becoming owners of the property or any part of it or otherwise) to participate in or receive profits or income arising from the acquisition, holding, management or disposal of the property or sums paid out of such profits or income.

(2)The arrangements must be such that the persons who are to participate ("participants") do not have day-to-day control over the management of the property, whether or not they have the right to be consulted or to give directions.

(3)The arrangements must also have either or both of the following characteristics—

(a)the contributions of the participants and the profits or income out of which payments are to be made to them are pooled;

(b)the property is managed as a whole by or on behalf of the operator of the scheme.

(4)If arrangements provide for such pooling as is mentioned in subsection (3)(a) in relation to separate parts of the property, the arrangements are not to be regarded as constituting a single collective investment scheme unless the participants are entitled to exchange rights in one part for rights in another.

(5)The Treasury may by order provide that arrangements do not amount to a collective investment scheme—

(a)in specified circumstances; or

(b)if the arrangements fall within a specified category of arrangement.

The Schedule to the FSMA 2000 (Collective Investment Schemes) Order 2001 (S.I. 2001/1062, "the CIS Order") specifies;

Arrangements Not Amounting to a Collective Investment Scheme.

1) Individual investment management arrangements, being a. investments of a kind specified in articles 76 to 81 of the FSMA 2000 Regulated Activities Order 2001 ("the RAO") or contracts of long-term insurance, provided that b. each participant is entitled to a part of that property and to withdraw that part at any time; and c. the arrangements do not have the characteristics mentioned in section 253(3) (a) of the statute and have those mentioned by section 253(3)(b) only because the parts of the property to which different participants are entitled are not bought and sold separately except where a person becomes or ceases to become a participant;

2) Enterprise initiative schemes;

3) Pure deposit based schemes;

4) Schemes not operated by way of business;

5) Debt issues, as defined in articles 76 to 79 of the RAO;

6) Common accounts;

7) Certain funds relating to leasehold property; LEGAL_DOCS:113688v2 24

8) Certain employee share schemes;

9) Schemes entered into for commercial purposes related to existing business;

10) Group schemes, i.e. schemes where participants are companies in the same group;

11) Franchise arrangements;

12) Trading schemes;

13) Timeshare schemes;

14) Other schemes relating to use or enjoyment of property;

15) Schemes involving the issue of certificates representing investments;

16) Clearing services;

17) Contracts of insurance;

18) Funeral plan contracts;

19) Individual pension accounts;

20) Occupational and personal pension schemes;

21) Bodies corporate etc. This exempts all companies other than open-ended investment companies, but the exclusion does not apply to any body incorporated as a limited liability partnership.

Review of Insolvency Practitioner Fees

Report to the Insolvency Service

Elaine Kempson

July 2013

Conclusions and proposals for change

The evidence provided to the review suggests that the current system of controls on IP remuneration works as intended where a secured creditor plays an active part in an insolvency. For the most part this applies to larger corporate insolvency cases. Here there is a degree of competition both for IPs wanting to join and remain on the banks' panels and, in some cases, a limited tendering process for individual jobs as well. Banks effectively act as a 'client' to whom the IP works. And there is effective ongoing oversight that the work is done efficiently and is effective and that the time charged is for work that is necessary and properly performed.

On the other hand, there is clear evidence that in a sizeable minority of cases, where control of the IP's remuneration and disbursements lies in the hands of unsecured creditors collectively, the current provisions through which they should exert that control are not working as intended. This occurs more commonly in corporate insolvencies than in personal bankruptcies in part because the creditors are much less likely to have experience of more than one insolvency.

In such circumstances there is very little real competition for jobs. There is also usually no identifiable 'client', and the IP will be working to the generality of unsecured creditors most of whom they will have very limited, if any, contact with beyond confirming their claim. Moreover, other than the small number of large unsecured creditors who account for more than 10 per cent of the estate, most have to work in conjunction with others they don't know and would find it difficult to contact.

In addition, there is usually no effective oversight by unsecured creditors of the work being undertaken by the IP or of the time being charged for it. A number of reasons have been identified for this, including: lack of engagement by creditors; the way fees are charged; shortcomings in existing Practice Notes and current limitations in compliance monitoring by regulatory bodies.

On the whole there is very limited engagement by unsecured creditors, few vote at creditors' meetings, even fewer attend these meetings in person and creditor committees are seldom set up. There are two main explanations for this low level of engagement: limited creditor knowledge and understanding which is compounded by the inadequacy of the information to creditors, and opportunity cost considerations. While this applies across all types of corporate insolvency, there are two circumstances where the legislation inhibits engagement by unsecured creditors. This includes administrations, where there is no requirement to hold a creditor meeting at the outset. It also applies to cases where it only becomes clear some time into a case that there is likely to be a distribution to unsecured creditors and the secured creditor, having been paid in full, ceases to exercise oversight. Even though oversight then passes to the unsecured creditors there is no requirement to hold a creditor meeting at that point.

The fact that the majority of cases are charged on time-cost basis means that a creditor needs considerable knowledge and skill to exercise oversight. Many of the unsecured creditors involved in corporate insolvencies lack both. And, because fees tend to be approved and drawn in stages as the case progresses, any knowledge and expertise an unsecured creditor may build up over the duration of a case could come too late to influence more than a small residue of fees. Moreover, the lack of fee estimates or fee caps at the outset of a case means that unsecured creditors cannot engage in any meaningful oversight until the time has been spent and they are consequently in the position of having to mount a challenge if they are not content. Other than the small number of large unsecured creditors who account for more than 10 per cent of the estate, most have to work in conjunction with others to do this. Moreover, there is only an eight-week window in which to do this.

The existing codes of practice and the associated regime for compliance monitoring is inadequate when it comes to remuneration. This means that independent oversight to ensure that time charged is for work that is necessarily and properly performed is largely absent. This leaves an unsecured creditor only with recourse to the courts. The costs and skill required act as a deterrent to them taking fee challenges to court.

There are also two sets of circumstances where safeguards for debtors and company directors seem inadequate. These include annulments of personal bankruptcies through the sale of the family home, where the original debt was for a very small sum, and company directors who have given a guarantee to a secured creditor who have no rights as contingent creditor until that guarantee is called in. Together these account for a

253

large proportion of the complaints that reach MPs and Ministers.

The review has received clear evidence that in circumstances where the controls *do* work, fees can be considerably lower. It shows that the OFT estimate of the size of this reduction (nine per cent) is probably conservative. In contrast, the OFT calculation that this applies to 37 per cent of cases may be an over-estimate.

Some very authoritive contributors to the review have been able to identify specific areas where successful challenges to fees are made. These include what overheads are covered by headline hourly rates, the way time is recorded, and failure to demonstrate that work undertaken was necessary, efficiently carried out or properly performed. It is important to note that these should not be (mis)interpreted as a deliberate intention to overcharge where controls are minimal or absent. But nor can it be interpreted as a free market working.

6.1 Proposals for change

Because, in general, secured creditors have systems of control that provide some degree of competition and strong oversight any changes should be limited to the (sizeable) minority of cases where control is intended to be exerted by unsecured creditors, particularly where no creditor committee has been set up. And although the focus is on corporate insolvency for the reasons outlined above, many of the suggestions made below would equally be of benefit in personal bankruptcy cases too. There is also a short section covering the situations where a personal debtor or company director will effectively be responsible for meeting the IP's remuneration and other disbursements and costs and where controls are either absent or not working as intended.

It is unlikely that a single change would deal with all the key issues that have been identified by this review. That will require changes in a number of areas in combination as outlined below.

6.1.1 Increasing competition

As the starting point is that there is evidence of market failure, the usual response would be to identify ways of stimulating greater competition. But, given the nature of the work undertaken by Insolvency Practitioners this is not an easy thing to achieve. Indeed, the Office of Fair Trading market review similarly concluded that there was market failure yet proposed only regulatory remedies.

In contrast, an enquiry by the Economic References Committee of the Australian Senate did explore market solutions in their report *'The regulation, registration and remuneration of insolvency practitioners in Australia: the case for a new framework'* that was published in September 2010. In this they considered the potential for competitive tendering when IPs are appointed to a case and concluded that although it would be *'appealing in principle'* it would be *'unreasonable given that the complexity of an insolvency job is often not apparent prior to an appointment'*.

In a subsequent judgement, Judge Finkelstein took *'a different view from that taken by the Senators'*. He identified a number of benefits of a competitive tendering process in the Australian context, including:

- It would secure the independence of the IP.

- Fees would be lower.

- More information would be made available to allow an assessment of whether or not fees are reasonable.

- The creation of opportunities for new IPs to enter the market.

- The prevention of cosy relationships being developed between IPs and creditors such as banks and finance companies and also between IPs and lawyers who refer work to each other.

At the same time, he also identified some 'downsides', although he did not feel that these outweighed the advantages above:

- Price competition could lead to lower quality work, with corners being cut to preserve profits.

- The difficulty of comparing bids on criteria other than price.

- The lack of an institution with the necessary skills to manage a tender process; the options he considered were the courts, the regulator (ASIC) and creditor committees.

- The shortage of IPs willing to bid against those known to deliver low-cost work but with low-quality .

- A tender process could be too slow for cases where an IP needs to be appointed swiftly.

These are very real concerns that may well rule out competition in the UK. Never-the-less the potential for limited competitive tendering in the UK is worthy of further consideration.

6.1.2 Information disclosure and transparency for creditors

The next option is to look at whether greater information disclosure and transparency could increase either competition or the ability of unsecured creditors to oversee and influence fees as the secured creditors are able to do. Here there are two main areas that need to be addressed:

- Information provided by the IP to creditors about the time spent on a case and fees charged.

- Information to help unsecured to assess whether those fees are reasonable.

Beginning with the information provided by the IP to creditors, it is common ground both inside and outside the insolvency profession that, over time, reports to creditors have become longer, more formulaic and less useful to creditors. Both submissions to the review and discussions at the subsequent round table identified this as an area where change is needed, with SIP9 needing radical revision or replacement. Moreover, creditors only receive any real information about the fees charged after those charges have been incurred and at the round table it was agreed that, where the IP is proposing that remuneration should be on a time-cost basis, creditors could and should be given an estimate of the costs at the outset of the case, alongside the headline rates. Here there is much that we can learn from Australia and from the Insolvency Practitioners Association of Australia

(IPAA) Code of Professional Practice in particular. This detailed document has three primary purposes:

- To set standards of conduct for insolvency professionals;

- To inform and educate IPA members as to the standards of conduct required of them in the discharge of their professional responsibilities; and

- To provide a reference for stakeholders against which they can gauge the conduct of IPA members.

It requires IPs to give creditors, at the time the method of remuneration is being agreed, information about the work that it is anticipated will need to be done and to agree a cap on fees (see section 6.1.4 below). This cap can only be increased by the IP returning to creditors with a detailed explanation of why it has been exceeded and full justification for the revised costing. The Code also contains detailed coverage of remuneration reporting, requiring IPs not only to account for the work done but also to show that it was undertaken efficiently and that the time spent was both necessary and work properly performed. It includes detailed examples illustrating where each of these criteria could not be considered to have been met and where work should not be charged to a case. These examples echo the grounds on which successful challenges are mounted to IPs fees in the UK. The Code is reinforced by a Remuneration Request Approval Report template sheet that sets out the format for the detailed reporting of both IP remuneration and disbursements and is more detailed than SIP9. This is in a format that would provide creditors with the information they need to exercise oversight, and would be easy to populate from records collated from timesheets completed by individual members of staff. A detailed Code of this kind would be very difficult to compile by committee and would require a single body, almost certainly the Insolvency Service in consultation with the insolvency profession, to do it. Once written, though, it could be used as part of a self-regulatory regime.

Such disclosure is only part of the information needed by creditors who, for the most part, will need some contextual information from an independent body to help them assess the reasonableness of the remuneration and disbursements being proposed . The Australian regulator (ASIC) has produced a helpful information sheet for unsecured creditors setting out how they should approach this task. They also publish detailed information on the fees charged each year for insolvencies of different types, by industrial sector, and by State. More detailed sets of tables are provided for each of the four industrial sectors accounting for the largest number of insolvencies plus one for all other insolvencies, which set out the levels of remuneration by type of insolvency within State. So, for example, a creditor can identify the range of fees charged in 2011/12 for the 109 liquidations involving construction firms in Western Australia.

Improved information in both of these areas (reporting by IPs and contextual information) would be especially helpful to the organisations who are regularly unsecured creditors in insolvency, for example local authorities, HMRC and the Institute of Credit Management. And both would be important even if there were more competition. For this reason, the Insolvency Service should explore the possibilities of following the Australian examples described above. Although the need is perhaps greatest for unsecured creditors in corporate insolvencies, it could be equally helpful for creditors in personal bankruptcies too.

6.1.3 Increasing unsecured creditor engagement

Even together greater information disclosure in these two areas would almost certainly not be sufficient to encourage many unsecured creditors in corporate insolvencies to become more engaged in the process. Limited creditor engagement in cases of corporate insolvency is not a problem that is peculiar to Britain. And even with the additional information disclosure described above, creditor engagement remains a problem in Australia.

In many jurisdictions, the Crown plays a much more active role in insolvencies where it is a creditor than is the case in the UK. The OFT market review concluded that HMRC should be more active as it is frequently a creditor in corporate insolvencies and often the unsecured creditor owed the largest sum of money. This was discussed at some length in the review round table where there was a widespread desire among all stakeholders for HMRC to play a greater role. However, given the current restrictions of departmental spending, HMRC is having to prioritise cases where there is evidence of potential dishonesty or fraud by company directors. In contrast, the Pension Protection Fund already plays an active oversight role and it might be expected that improved information disclosure would allow them to be more active still. But, unlike HMRC, they are a creditor in only a minority of insolvencies. By working together the two Crown creditors (HMRC and the Redundancy Payments Service) and the Pension Protection Fund could provide effective oversight of cases where the IP fees are above a minimum threshold. While their involvement would not solve the problem of creditor engagement generally it would ensure that oversight was exercised that would be in the interest of unsecured creditors as a whole. For this reason, the Insolvency Service should convene a meeting of the representative of HMRC, the Redundancy Payments Service and the Pension Protection Fund to discuss how, between them, they could exercise greater oversight. In time, the cost of oversight could be covered, in part if not in full, by the increased dividends received. But if resources would be required for the Crown to play a more active role, the potential should be investigated for allocating unclaimed, indivisible account and reserve fund monies from insolvencies, that are currently returned to HM Treasury. Lessons might be learnt from the Big Society Trust, which is financed by money that is released for social spending through the Dormant Accounts Scheme.

In Austria, lack of individual creditor engagement has been overcome through the creation of commercial bodies that represent creditors collectively. There are four creditor protection associations that are privileged under Austrian bankruptcy law. They may request information and file appeals during pre-bankruptcy proceedings and can become members of the creditors' committee, which supervises and supports the trustee in bankruptcy in complex insolvency cases. These associations have been in existence for between 20 and 25 years, and evolved out of organisations providing debt recovery services for creditors . They are now an important part of the insolvency world, representing the interests of small unsecured creditors who would, in other jurisdictions, almost certainly play no role in the insolvency proceedings. When an insolvency case goes to the court the associations have access to the list of the creditors involved so that they can write to them to offer their services. Creditors accepting the offer will pay a small fee (usually €100 to 300, depending on the amount of money they are owed) for which the association will establish their claim against the estate and represent the creditor (along with others also becoming their clients) throughout the insolvency proceedings. This includes sitting on any creditor committee that is set up.   As a member of a committee, the associations will, collectively, also a receive a fee that is a percentage of the fee that is paid to the Insolvency Practitioner at the end of the case; 10 per cent for an insolvency , but 15 per cent for a 're-organisation' (roughly equivalent to an IVA or CVA) . This is divided among the associations involved in an insolvency *pro rata* to the creditors they represent. It should, however, be noted that, in Austria, Insolvency Practitioners' remuneration is a set percentage of realisations, with two sliding scales, one for the secured debts and one for unsecured, and linked to the level of assets realised.   So the role of the creditor protection associations is somewhat simplified.   Never-the-less, the role they play is broadly similar to the role played in IVAs by organisations such as TDX. The key differences being that their role is recognised by legislation and the courts and the formula by which they are paid, which makes it possible for them to represent small trade creditors. This is a model that is worthy of closer scrutiny to see how transferable it would be to the UK context and what changes to the UK regime, if any, would be required to make it more transferable. In doing so, lessons might usefully be learnt from the experiences in Germany where similar organisations have recently been set up.

Germany has, in fact, taken several steps to encourage greater creditor involvement. Creditors who sit on committees are paid a modest fee for their input, which would address the opportunity cost disincentive identified in this review. Even so creditors' committees are estimated to be established in just 15-20 per cent of cases. The 2012 Reform Act on insolvency in Germany directly addresses the issue of creditor engagement and obliges the court to set up a preliminary creditors committee if requested to do so by either a creditor or the debtor. This excludes insolvencies of small firms and to qualify the insolvent company should have reached at least two of the following three thresholds in the preceding business year:

- A balance sheet of €4.84 million (after the deduction of negative equity)
- A revenue of €9.68 million, and
- 50 employees.

The court may, however, refuse to appoint a preliminary committee if the business has stopped trading; the appointment would lead to significant delays that would have an adverse effect on the financial situation of the insolvent company, or the appointment would be too costly relative to the expected insolvency estate.

The new regime anticipates that the following creditor groups will be represented on the committee: secured creditors; creditors with the highest claims; creditors with smaller claims and employee representatives. Participation is not, however, obligatory. The primary purpose of the committee is to appoint the insolvency practitioner, and not the oversight of work done or levels of remuneration.

So far the focus has been on ensuring that creditors engage where they have a right to do so. But there are two sets of circumstances where unsecured creditors have limited opportunities for engagement. These are in administrations, where there is no requirement for an IP to hold a meeting at the outset, and cases where it becomes clear that the secured creditor(s) will be paid in full and oversight responsibility passes to the unsecured creditors although there is no requirement to call a creditor meeting. These are both areas that merit reconsideration to see if more control can be given to unsecured creditors.

6.1.4 Simplifying the process of oversight by unsecured creditors

Where remuneration is based on a time-cost basis, with only the hourly rate known in advance, a creditor needs considerable expertise to oversee cases and engage in a meaningful discussion of the work done and the level of fees and disbursements charged for it. In fact the organisations that do provide this oversight generally have staff who are trained IPs to undertake it. This is an expensive resource and one that only the creditors who are regularly involved in insolvencies and are owed large sums of money could justify.

The other option would be to simplify the oversight needed by looking again at the way that fees are determined. Section 6.1.2 above raised the issue of providing estimates of likely costs at the outset of a case,

264

along with a detailed explanation of what can be done for this money. This would be a considerable advantage for the larger unsecured creditors, especially if it were married with a fee cap and a need to return to creditors to justify and seek approval of additional fees (as in Australia).

A more radical change in the basis for remuneration could make oversight easier still. In some jurisdictions the main or only method of setting an IP's remuneration is as a percentage of realisations (and this was also much more common in UK in the past). Moving to this as the presumed method for setting remuneration in the UK would, however, be problematic as creditors currently have responsibility for setting the percentage and they lack the knowledge and skills to determine the rate that would be appropriate in a particular case. Change in this area would almost certainly require a more nuanced approach, with a statutory scale that links the percentage to the level of assets realised to ensure that IPs would be prepared to take on cases where realisations are likely to be low. And, as in Austria, there would need to be separate scales for the secured and unsecured assets.

A more promising approach may lie in the 2010 Insolvency (Amendment) Rules, which allow for different methods of charging for different aspects of a case. These appear to have been little used by IPs. This is an area that should be explored further, for example fixed fees for statutory duties; a percentage of realisations for asset realisations (with a statutory sliding scale as described above); perhaps retaining time cost for investigations. This could greatly limit the amounts of remuneration over which unsecured creditors would need to exercise oversight. And in doing so it could also limit the number of complaints relating to fees and increase levels of confidence in the profession.

6.1.5 Safeguards for personal debtors and company directors

Before 2010 people made bankrupt had no explicit right to challenge fees. Since that date a bankrupt can apply to court for permission to challenge their trustee's fees, provided they can demonstrate that there is or is likely to be a surplus of assets available to the bankrupt – or there would be a surplus but for the fees charged by the IP. As discussed in section 4.3, improved safeguards may be required for personal debtors seeking an annulment through the sale of the family home (or where the home has to be sold to realise assets to clear the debts). It is clear from the evidence received in this review that the IP's remuneration and associated disbursements can be considerably larger than the debt that gave rise to the bankruptcy.   There are a number of reasons for this each of which needs to be addressed.

First, there is the lower limit (currently £750) of the size of the debt for which someone can be made bankrupt. It has been at this level since the Insolvency Act 1986 and is now far less than either the petitioning creditor fees (of around £3,000) or the Official Receiver fee (£1,715) and equates to only two to three hours of an IP's time. There is a very strong case for increasing the threshold to a figure that at the very least covers the creditor and court fees. In addition, consideration could be given to amending section 273 of the Insolvency Act to cover creditor petitions for bankruptcy as well as debtor petitions. This allows the court to refer a debtor with a low level of debt to an IP for a review of their circumstances to assess whether another course of action would be more appropriate than personal bankruptcy.

Secondly, personal debtors have a very poor understanding of the costs they will incur as a consequence of being made bankrupt. Nor do they understand the work that an IP will, properly, need to do or that their failure to co-operate with the IP will inevitably lead to higher fees. Where they are in contact with one of the not-for-profit debt advice agencies this will be explained, but debtors who are not will have a very poor understanding indeed. There is, therefore, a case for the Insolvency Service producing an information sheet that spells these points out and for creditors to be required to make debtors fully aware of the facts before they initiate bankruptcy proceedings.

Finally, cases do reach the courts where the level of the IP's remuneration cannot be justified to the court's satisfaction. Where creditors no longer have any incentive to scrutinise the fees charged, because the assets being realised greatly exceed the money they are owed, it is unlikely that the debtor will have the knowledge required to do so in a productive way. Independent oversight seems the most likely alternative in such cases and this is discussed below. The Official Receiver taking responsibility for these cases is, however, another possibility

Turning now to company directors in smaller corporate insolvencies who have given a personal guarantee to a secured creditor, here the issue also focuses on the IP's fees but is in reality more complex. As with the personal debtors, better information would undoubtedly help and the Insolvency Service should consider producing information materials explaining to directors in this position that they will not have rights as a 'creditor' until such times as they are responsible for the debt when the bank calls in the guarantee. This should also spell out the importance of co-operating with the IP to avoid needless work and fees. In addition, there is no reason currently why directors in this position should not receive all the information that is given to the company's creditors to keep them fully informed and IPs should be required to do so, along with an explanation of the directors' rights.

At the same time, there is a need for banks and others taking security in the form of a personal guarantee to recognise that there is a moral, if not a legal, requirement for them to keep the director involved and to listen to any concerns they may have about the appropriateness and effectiveness of any work that is being done by the IP. Cases were provided in evidence to this review showing that this does not always happen.

6.1.6 Enhanced monitoring by regulator(s)

As discussed above (section 6.1.2), there is a need for a more extensive Code of Practice, similar to the one in Australia. This would, in turn open up the possibility of a greater degree of compliance monitoring of fees in both corporate insolvencies and in personal bankruptcies than is currently the case. In the absence of a competitive market or effective oversight by unsecured creditors, this is particularly important both for the reputation of the profession and to ensure that work is properly undertaken and levels of remuneration are appropriate.

The information provided to this review does, however, show a considerable variation in the level of compliance monitoring currently undertaken by the RPBs. This is, perhaps the inevitable consequence of having so many bodies acting as regulators. There is certainly a case to be made for reducing the number of RPBs by setting a minimum threshold for the number of IPs that they regulate. Ultimately there is a case for a single regulator - and perhaps even for bringing the profession under the Financial Conduct Authority, just as Australian IPs are regulated by the equivalent body, the Australian Securities and Investments Commission (ASIC).

For as long as there continues to be a number of (self) regulatory bodies, the Insolvency Service needs to play an active role in ensuring that they operate to common standards of compliance monitoring and enforcement.

6.1.7 Simple, low-cost mediation and adjudication service for fee disputes

The starting point for any changes and reforms should be on providing greater oversight and, therefore, reducing the numbers of complaints and challenges relating to fees.

Even so, there will always be unresolved issues relating to fees, often in cases where the fees are low and the costs of a full court hearing would be disproportionate. This suggests the need for a simple, low-cost mediation and adjudication service for disputes about low-level fees, leaving the courts free to deal with the cases involving larger sums of money. This is not a new suggestion. The OFT made a similar recommendation in their market review report as did a report of research undertaken for the Insolvency Practices Council. It was also suggested and discussed by participants in the review round table. The simplest way of achieving this would be to extend the jurisdiction of the Financial Ombudsman Service, which already covers debt management companies and debt advice agencies. The feasibility of achieving this should be explored.

6.1.8 Independent oversight of fees

If it is not possible to achieve reforms in each of the areas in sections 6.1.1 to 6.1.6 above then consideration will need to be given to some form of independent oversight. This would apply to cases where oversight currently falls to unsecured creditors and no creditors' committee has been set up and also for cases where the assets realised in a personal bankruptcy are greatly in excess of the amounts owed to creditors such that they have no incentive to oversee the IP fees being charged.

Such oversight already exists in Scotland in the form of court reporters for corporate insolvency (IPs who scrutinise the work undertaken and fees charged by their peers on behalf of the court) and the Accountant in Bankruptcy for personal bankruptcies.

JULY 2008

FINANCIAL MARKETS LAW
COMMITTEE

ISSUE 86 - "OPERATING" A
COLLECTIVE INVESTMENT SCHEME

*Legal assessment of
problems associated with
the definition of Collective
Investment Scheme and
related terms*

Authors:

| Michael Brindle QC | Fountain |
| Court Chambers | |

| Richard Stones | Lovells |
| LLP | |

Editorial support:

Joanna Perkins Secretary, FMLC

| Saima Hanif | Legal |
| Assistant, FMLC | |

| Kate Morris | Legal |
| Assistant, FMLC | |

| Danai Azaria | Legal |
| Intern, FMLC | |

| Chinonyelum Uwazie | Legal |
| Intern, FMLC | |

CONTENTS

272

1 INTRODUCTION AND EXECUTIVE SUMMARY

a) Introduction

1.1 The role of the Financial Markets Law Committee ("FMLC") is to identify issues of legal uncertainty, or misunderstanding, present and future, in the framework of the wholesale financial markets which might give rise to material risks and to consider how such issues should be addressed.

1.2 In February 2004, a number of uncertainties in the legal and regulatory framework relating to the operation of a collective investment scheme ("CIS") were brought to the Committee's attention by market contacts. In November 2005, the Court of Appeal in FSA v. Fradley and Woodward2 delivered a judgment relevant to the operation of a CIS in the UK. Market contacts expressed their concern to the FMLC that the judgment had set an unexpectedly low threshold in determining when a manager is operating a CIS. In 2006, the FMLC investigated these concerns by consulting experts in the field. In the course of these enquiries it became apparent that not only did the criteria for establishing a CIS create legal uncertainty, but a number of other questions relating to CISs were raised, especially in view of the Treasury's proposal to amend paragraph

273

9 of the Schedule to the FSMA 2000 (Collective Investment Schemes) Order 2001 ("CIS Order"). Further consultation on the proposed amendment of paragraph 9 ensued, and the Treasury's amendments were implemented in final form by the FSMA 2000 (Collective Investment Schemes) (Amendment) Order 20083. Nonetheless a number of problems remain unresolved. This paper now provides a comprehensive account of some of the key issues examined by the FMLC and sets out an analysis of those issues, providing a legal assessment of the problems arising.

Executive Summary

Section 235 of the Financial Services and Markets Act 2000 ("FSMA") sets out the elements of a CIS. There is uncertainty in the meaning and effect of those elements. The greatest problems lie with the wide concept of "arrangements" (including the problem of the management of property "as a whole") and the uncertainties in relation to "day to day control" and the meaning of "operator".

The market in the UK is aware of the issues highlighted in this paper and has come up with structures to counter the associated difficulties, but an improvement to the definition of a CIS would nonetheless be much welcomed. The ambit of the statute could easily be clarified without the concept of a CIS becoming undesirably restricted.

Amendment to the exclusions contained in the Schedule to the CIS Order may ameliorate the problems and is to be welcomed, especially in relation to paragraph 9. However, this is not in our view a substitute for the need to clarify the definitions in section 235 of FSMA.

OVERVIEW OF THE LEGAL UNCERTAINTY ISSUES ARISING IN CONNECTION WITH THE DEFINITION OF CIS

Implications of the definition

Because of the regulatory consequences stemming from a scheme qualifying as CIS, legal uncertainty arising in the context of such definition affects the efficient application of the regulatory regime and concomitantly the operation of the financial markets. The key regulatory aspects of CISs are summarised below:

The establishment, operation and winding up of a CIS are regulated activities under the FSMA 2000 (Regulated Activities) Order 2001 (S.I. 2001/544, the "RAO").4 This means that any person carrying on the business of doing so needs to obtain permission from the FSA under Part IV of the FSMA. Failure to do so is a serious criminal offence, and the FSA has extensive powers of intervention to prevent the prohibition from being contravened.

Once authorised, there are significant regulatory restrictions on the ability of a CIS to invest and in particular to acquire certain assets, for example derivatives.5

Agreements entered into by a person in the course of carrying on a regulated activity without permission are unenforceable unless the court determines otherwise.6 This will primarily affect agreements between the person operating the putative CIS and the CIS itself or its participants, but could arguably (and more significantly) also apply to agreements which are entered into by the operator on behalf of the scheme.

There are considerable restrictions on the promotion of CISs (s238(1) FSMA). Unless a CIS is of a kind authorised or recognised under FSMA, it cannot be marketed except to certain specific categories of people, even if the communication is made or approved by an authorised person.7

A separate issue is tax. The FSMA definition of CIS is used in a variety of tax legislation relating both to stamp taxes and to taxes on income and capital gains. The tax treatment of a structure will often critically depend on whether it is or is not a CIS. In the tax area uncertainty in the definition is even more damaging than in the regulatory context. This is both because of the potentially unlimited financial consequences of a determination that a particular tax treatment is incorrect; and also because any pragmatic approach which may be adopted by the

FSA in the regulatory context is strictly irrelevant to the construction of the tax legislation. For example, guidance issued by the FSA (e.g. in its Perimeter Guidance Manual) is not binding on the courts.

Legal uncertainty in the definition of CIS

Section 235(1) of FSMA provides a very wide definition of a CIS, the main elements of which are discussed in section 3 below, starting with the wide concept of "arrangements", which is fully analysed in section 4 below. The provisions in FSMA, in the RAO and in the Schedule to the CIS Order have some, albeit limited, effect of limiting the wide scope of the definition set out in section 235(1).

Section 235(2) of FSMA refers to the notion of "day-to-day" control; this creates significant uncertainties in the interpretation and application of the CIS regime. The arrangement must be such that the participants do not have day-to- day control over the management of the property, whether or not they have the right to be consulted or to give directions. Several comments need to be made with respect to this definition.

The notion of "day to day control" is vague and FSMA does not give any further guidance on how it should be interpreted. Furthermore, the phrase "whether or not they have the right to be consulted or to give directions", which purports to clarify the "day to day control of the property" notion, is also obscure. There is not a clear picture as to which level of control the "right to be consulted or to give directions" encompasses.

Laddie J held in The Russell –Cooke Trust Company v. Elliott9 that a scheme is a CIS even if not all the participants in it have transferred day-to-day control of the management of their monies to the operators of the scheme. Based on this argument, Lady Justice Arden continued in Fradley that, for the purposes of that case, it did "not matter that the scheme was not a CIS as regards any participant who retained day-to-day control of the management of his monies".10

Section 235(2) of FSMA raises a question with regard to which actions may be considered to be "day-to-day control" by the participants. Do those actions need to be joint, or generally undertaken by all or more than one participants? In Fradley, Lady Justice Arden reasoned with respect to the word "operator" in section 235 of FSMA that "the singular in a statute includes the plural".11 But does the plural include the singular in respect of participants? The interplay between operator and participants is considered in sections 5 and 6 below.

Section 235(5) empowers the Treasury ("HMT") to provide by order that certain arrangements do not amount to CISs in two cases: (a) in specified circumstances or (b) if the arrangements fall within a specified category of arrangements. The wording of this provision allows HMT to exercise a certain degree of discretionary power, which may raise uncertainty, since the "specified circumstances" could encompass an unexpectedly wide range of conditions.

Article 3 and the Schedule of the CIS Order, as in force since 1 December 2001, set out the arrangements which do not amount to CISs. The list is extensive and could pose problems for the market participants to know the state of the law. It has been suggested that some of the issues discussed below could be solved by extending the exclusions. However, it is arguable that the adding of further exclusions to a very wide basic definition of CIS could worsen the present state of play. The exclusions are considered in section 7 below.

The market in the UK is already aware of the issues highlighted above and has come up with structures to counter the associated difficulties, but an improvement to the definition of a CIS is nevertheless important, especially for those who need advice as to whether schemes which they propose qualify as CIS schemes or not.

THE DEFINITION OF A CIS

Section 235 FSMA defines a CIS as follows:

In this Part "collective investment scheme" means any arrangements with respect to property of any description, including money, the purpose or effect of which is to enable persons taking part in the arrangements (whether by becoming owners of the property or any part of it or otherwise) to participate in or receive profits or income arising from the acquisition, holding, management or disposal of the property or sums paid out of such profits or income.

The arrangements must be such that the persons who are to participate ("participants") do not have day-to-day control over the management of the property, whether or not they have the right to be consulted or to give directions.

The arrangements must also have either or both of the following characteristics—

    i)   the contributions of the participants and the profits or income out of which payments are to be made to them are pooled;

    ii)   the property is managed as a whole by or on behalf of the operator of the scheme.

If arrangements provide for such pooling as is mentioned in subsection (3)(a) in relation to separate parts of the property, the arrangements are not to be regarded as constituting a single collective investment scheme unless the participants are entitled to exchange rights in one part for rights in another.

The Treasury may by order provide that arrangements do not amount to a collective investment scheme—

in specified circumstances; or if the arrangements fall within a specified category of arrangement.

The definitions in section 235 FSMA comprise the following key elements:

a general description of the type of "arrangements" which are capable of falling with the definition (section 235(1));

additional criteria which must be satisfied by such arrangements:

the test of "day to day control of management" (section 235(2));

the alternative tests of "pooling" and "management of the property as a whole" (section 235(3)).

These are analysed briefly in turn, so that the essential problems within the definition can be understood. The problem areas are analysed more fully in later chapters.

Arrangements

The "arrangements" within section 235(1) are:

arrangements with respect to property of any description, including money, the purpose or effect of which is to enable persons taking part in the arrangements (whether by becoming owners of the property or any part of it or otherwise) to participate in or receive profits or income arising from the acquisition, holding, management or disposal of the property or sums paid out of such profits or income.

The scope of this definition is clearly very wide. In particular:

"arrangements" is a very broad term, and arrangements may have no clear boundaries. So, for example, a series of separate trusts may be viewed as a single set of "arrangements" (as in Elliott); on the other hand it is quite possible that a single financial structure may be analysed as comprising a series of separate or overlapping sets of "arrangements";

the arrangements may apply to "property of any description" and are not restricted to "investments" within the meaning of the RAO. A CIS can relate to, for example, real estate, rights under betting contracts or even to ostriches;

there is no need for the participants to have any ownership or other interest in the property, or to receive directly the profits or income arising from its management. So, to take merely one example, an insurance company selling with profits policies would fall within the definition in the absence of exemption;

arrangements can be caught if their "purpose" is to enable those taking part to participate in the relevant profits or income, even if this is not achieved; and conversely where this is the "effect" of the arrangements, even if this is not their purpose, or primary purpose.

The breadth of the definition is clearly intentional: the aim is to cast the regulatory net wide and then cut back its scope with exclusions. The difficulty with this approach is that:

it leaves within the net harmless arrangements where the need for an exclusion has not been identified; more insidiously, the generality of the definition may be expansively interpreted by reference to the exclusions.

More specific uncertainty relates to what is meant by "persons taking part in the arrangements". It is at least arguable that this phrase implies a degree of positive involvement (so that, for example a private trust, or a fund designed to compensate or make charitable payments to specified categories of beneficiaries, will not be caught). However, this is only one view. A related question is whether it is of the essence that the persons concerned make a financial contribution: this might be inferred from the reference to "the contributions of the participants" in section 235(3)(a) but this also is far from conclusive.

Day-to-day control over management

To qualify as a CIS the arrangements discussed above must have the additional characteristic that they are:

such that the persons who are to participate ("participants") do not have day-to-day control over the management of the property, whether or not they have the right to be consulted or to give directions." (Section 253(2)).

"Day-to-day control over the management of…" is not a wholly easy concept. "Control over the management of…" is presumably intended to be distinguished from "management of…" i.e. arrangements will not qualify simply because the participants do not manage the property themselves. On the other hand "day to day control" must clearly mean more than having the "right to be consulted or to give directions". In Elliott, Laddie J referred "in colloquial terms" to "minding the shop". In practice it is not always easy to apply the test, though it appears that as a minimum the participants should be in a position to tell the person who is actually managing the property what to do on a continuing day-to-day basis.

More specifically:

it is difficult to apply the test to property which requires only occasional "management" or no "management" at all, e.g. a portfolio of fixed term debt securities;

it is established that the test is whether all the participants have "day-to- day control". But it is unclear whether this means the participants collectively (in which case some participants could possibly have more control than others) or individually. If the latter is right, it is hard to see

how arrangements with more than a very small number of participants could ever satisfy the test.

Pooling

The test in section 253(3)(a) is that:

"the contributions of the participants and the profits or income out of which payments are to be made to them are pooled".

This does not seem to give to any particular problems, except to the extent that some or all of the participants do not make "contributions" at all. We therefore do not consider this point further in this paper.

Management of the property "as a whole"

Section 235(3)(b) requires that (if the pooling criterion is not met) the property concerned must be "must be managed as a whole by or on behalf of the operator of the scheme".

This criterion, and the contrast with the alternative of "pooling", makes it clear that arrangements can (in the absence of an exclusion) amount to a CIS even though each participant is entitled to distinct part of the property if all such property is "managed as a whole". Take the example of an asset manager which provides a "managed fund service", i.e. buys and sells units in investment funds for its clients on the basis of preset models depending on the client's risk appetite: all clients with the same risk appetite will hold investments of the same kind in the same proportions, even though these may be held in separate accounts beneficially owned by the individual clients. It is arguable that notwithstanding the distinct entitlements the "arrangements" under which they are managed may fall within the CIS definition. This view issupported by the existence of a partial exclusion for "individual investment management assignments".

However in such cases it may be possible to argue:

that the "arrangements" do not "enable" the participant to invest (as required by section 235(1)), since the manager could have provided the same result by managing each investor's portfolio entirely separately; or

more generally, on a purposive basis, that the arrangements have no "communal" basis: in Elliott Laddie J felt able to exclude from the scope of a putative CIS arrangements under which the clients chose their own investments, on the broad grounds that "the arrangements put in place and given effect to were not for the purpose of enabling communal investment nor did they have that effect".

It is hard to take this any further. It seems to us to be an unnecessary element of uncertainty which could be easily clarified.

Who is "the operator"?

Section 235(3)(b) also raises the issue of what is meant by the "operator" of a CIS. "Operator" and "operate" are not defined generally in FSMA. Section

237 states that in relation to a unit trust scheme with a separate trustee, "operator" means the manager and that in relation to an open ended investment company it means that company. It is not clear how far these stipulations assist in interpreting the wider meaning of "operator", since they are probably based on a policy desire to prescribe who the operator is in the particular cases, rather starting from the general meaning of the term.

In the absence of any clear definition the key area of dispute in practice is whether "operation" extends to the overall "running" of the CIS, including the management of its assets (this is understood to be the view of the FSA); or is limited to the "administrative" aspects of operation (including in particular the accounting and calculations involved in the "collective" nature of the structure) to the exclusion of asset management.

The distinction is particularly important in funding structures (particularly limited partnerships) where separate entities perform the asset management and administrative functions. If the view in (a) is correct, both entities may be regarded as "operating" and will need to be authorised under FSMA. On the view in (b), the asset manager will not need authorisation as an "operator" and may not need authorisation at all if the assets concerned are not themselves "investments" within the meaning of the RAO.

There is one final difficulty. Where a CIS takes the form of a corporate body, it is unclear whether the entity is to be treated as "operating" itself or whether one should look beyond the entity to its management. In the original legislation this issue did not arise in practice, since: in the case of an open-ended investment company, the operator was defined as meaning the company (section 237) no other body corporate could constitute a CIS.

However the legislation was amended in an anomalous way to reflect the introduction of limited liability partnerships: an LLP can constitute a CIS, but there is no prescription as to who the operator will be in such a case.

It seems that the greatest problems lie with the wide concept of "arrangements" (including the problem of the management of property "as a whole") and the uncertainties in relation to "day to day control" and "operator". Each of these is considered separately below.

ARRANGEMENTS

In Fradley Lady Justice Arden said this (at paragraph 33):

The word "arrangements" has been considered in other statutory contexts. No formality is required. In some contexts communications may amount to "arrangements" even if they are not legally binding (see for example Re Duckwari PLC [1999] Ch 235 at 260). I need not decide whether that is the case in section 235. In my judgment, the judge was correct to say that "property of any description" in section 235(1) could include amounts paid to TBPS by persons joining in the scheme. There is no requirement for those monies to be invested in some investment....

She continued at paragraph 37 as follows:

…it is convenient to refer to a single set of "arrangement" as a single scheme. There is no doubt that the expression "operator" in section 235 includes two or more operators acting as operators of a single scheme: the singular in a statute includes the plural. Likewise, there is no logical reason why, if there are two operators, they should have to be responsible for the entire operation of the scheme. It is enough that they are responsible for separate parts of the entire scheme. But, where two services are offered together, it does not necessarily follow that there was only one set of arrangements.

With respect we do not find this at all clear. It is very hard for anyone advising those setting up what might be a collective investment scheme to give a conclusive opinion as to whether a set of arrangements will be regarded as a one "arrangement" or as several. We fully understand that it is the deliberate intention of the drafting of this legislation that it should cast as wide a net as possible, clawing back from that through a series of exemptions or exclusions. We also acknowledge that in many instances this may work reasonably satisfactorily, but sometimes this is not the case

As mentioned in section 3 above the Elliott decision supports the view that a series of separate trusts may be viewed as a single set of arrangements, whereas on the facts of Fradley it was regarded by the Court of Appeal as quite possible that a single financial structure could be analysed as comprising a series of separate and overlapping sets of arrangements. It is not very helpful to say that each case depends on its own individual facts

A further problem arises in connection with the reference in section 235(1) to "persons taking part in the arrangements". It is by no means clear how far this reaches. Does it only include those who have a degree of positive involvement, or does it include passive beneficiaries? In particular, how is a private trust to be treated? The definition, being intended to be wide, may well include anyone who stands to benefit from the arrangements, or it may require that they should do something in order to be said to participate. The reference in section 253(3) (a) to the contributions of participants suggests that at least some form of financial contribution may be required, but the logic for this requirement in the overall context of the statute is doubtful.

DAY TO DAY CONTROL

For a scheme to qualify as a CIS the "participants" must not have "day to day control over the management of the property, whether or not they have the right to be consulted or give directions". These words were considered in both Elliott and Fradley.

In Elliott Mr. Justice Laddie said that it is not necessary for all the participants in a CIS to have handed over day-to-day control over management of the property in order for the scheme to remain a CIS.

Thus, where some have transferred control and others have not, the scheme will be a CIS.

This was followed by the Court of Appeal in Fradley. At paragraph 46, Lady Justice Arden said:

…As Laddie J, held in…Elliott… a scheme will be a CIS even if not all the participants in it have transferred day-to-day control of the management of their monies to the operators of the scheme. This is because the fact that some of them have relinquished day-to-day control to the operators of the scheme means that section 235(2) is satisfied as regards them.

Nonetheless, confusion remains as to whether the same scheme can be regarded as a single uniform CIS from the different perspectives of both the participants who have relinquished day to day control and those who have not. In Elliott the view of Mr Justice Laddie was that if an investor who retains managerial control participates in an arrangement in which the other participants have relinquished control, it is just as much a CIS for him as it is for the others.

However, in Fradley Lady Justice Arden apparently took a different view. Following the dictum above, she went on to say:

That is sufficient for the purposes of this case; it does not matter that the scheme was not a CIS as regards any participant who retained day-to-day control of the management of his monies…

Thus, following Fradley, the position seems to be a curious one. A scheme can be a CIS and not a CIS at one and the same time, depending on which participant is under consideration. This can create difficulties of application of the requirements and benefits of being a CIS which are listed in paragraph 2.1 above. It also leads to the question whether the test is to be applied on a collective or an individual basis, a point not resolved by Elliott or Fradley. Perhaps either will suffice to take participants out of a CIS, even if others with neither form of control stay in. But if individual control is required to be outside the definition of a CIS, then there will rarely be a scheme which does not qualify as a CIS by virtue of section 235(2).

The word used in the sub-section is "participants". The use of the plural may indicate that an individual approach is not to be taken, but we are not convinced that this is correct. The plural could include the singular, and "participants" could mean "each participant, whether collectively or individually". One does not know the answer.

Nor is it clear what "day-to-day control" actually involves. Is this what the operator does or something else? Presumably control exercised on a weekly basis is not covered. The phrase "whether or not they have the right to be consulted or to give directions" does not assist. In particular, it is very unclear where the boundary lies between giving directions and having day to day control. To be in a position to give directions necessarily involves control, so the key is what is meant by "day-to-day". What of participants who give directions on a regular basis, perhaps daily or at least on many days? Is that giving directions or is that day-to-day control?

It may be that section 235(2) is drawing a distinction between the right to exercise control and the actual exercise of such rights. The mere right to give directions, even on a daily basis, does not constitute day-to-day control, but if the right is actually exercised on a regular basis it may do so. Once again, one cannot have any confidence in the correct answer to the question. The uncertainty is an inevitable consequence of the desire to caste the net as wide as possible. As with the other points considered in this paper, the ambit of the statute could easily be clarified without the definition of a CIS becoming undesirably restricted.

OPERATOR

The most important area of uncertainty in section 235 relates to the meaning of the expression "operator". Neither the word "operator" nor indeed "operate" are defined anywhere in FSMA.

Nonetheless, section 235(3) stipulates that a scheme can only be a CIS, where contributions and profits are not pooled if "the property is managed as a whole by or on behalf of the operator of the scheme". The question of what is management as a whole has been considered in section 3 above. But it is crucial to know whether such management is or is not "by or on behalf of the operator".

Section 237 does provide that in relation to a unit trust scheme with a separate trustee "operator" means the manager, and that in relation to an open-ended investment company it means that company. But these particular cases require that as a matter of policy it should be stipulated who the operator is; no clue at all is given as to the meaning of the expression in other situations.

There is a practical issue here as to which of the following is covered, or whether both are covered. Thus: does the operation refer to the actual running of the investment scheme, including the management of the assets themselves, or is operation a reference to administration of the scheme?

It is common for schemes to have an administrator, who deals with information and accounting, the valuation of interests, the calculation of payments due on exit from the scheme etc. Asset managers typically fulfil a different function. Section 235 (3) talks of management of the property by the operator, so that one might think that management of the assets is what the "operator" is concerned with, and it is believed that the Financial Services Authority is of the view that paragraph 6.4 (a) above is the correct view. But this is itself not certain.

The issue is of real practical importance in those cases where asset management and administration are separated. Do both asset manager and administrator have to manage the property as a whole? Is it enough if one or the other does so? If only (a) or (b) is covered, but not both, these questions can be answered, but which is it, (a) or (b)? And what of the custodian of the assets under a scheme, often a different party again from the administrator and the asset manager? Is he also an operator?

As with the observation in relation to "arrangements" and "day-to-day control", there is no obvious reason why these doubts could not be clarified without jeopardising the desire to cast the net wide. This would bring clarity where it is much needed for those operating in the financial markets.

One further point should be mentioned. Where a CIS is itself a corporate body, is that body to be regarded as "operating " itself, or need one look to who is managing within that body? The asset management and administration functions may all be functions of the company, but conducted by different individuals or groups of individuals. Again, who is the "operator"? This was foreseen in FSMA in relation to open-ended investment companies (see section 237), and no other body corporate could qualify as a CIS by virtue of paragraph 21 of the Schedule to the

CIS Order. However, that paragraph also provides that a limited liability partnership can constitute a CIS, without stipulating who the operator would be in such a case. Is the position the same as for an open- ended investment company? Again, this can readily be clarified.

EXCLUSIONS

As mentioned above, the statute, namely FSMA, defines a CIS very widely and then cuts it down by exclusions. We now turn to consider, without prejudice to our view that the statutory scope should be clarified as set out in sections 3 to 6 above, (a) what those exclusions are and any particular difficulties which arise with them and (b) whether or not those exclusions should be amended or extended.

The existing exclusions

The Schedule to the FSMA 2000 (Collective Investment Schemes) Order 2001 (S.I. 2001/1062, "the CIS Order") specifies arrangements not amounting to a collective investment scheme. These are:

Individual investment management arrangements, being

investments of a kind specified in articles 76 to 81 of the FSMA 2000 Regulated Activities Order 2001 ("the RAO") or contracts of long-term insurance, provided that each participant is entitled to a part of that property and to withdraw that part at any time; and the arrangements do not have the characteristics mentioned in section 253(3) (a) of the statute and have those mentioned by section 253(3)(b) only because the parts of the property to which different participants are entitled are not bought and sold separately except where a person becomes or ceases to become a participant;

Enterprise initiative schemes;

Pure deposit based schemes;

Schemes not operated by way of business;

Debt issues, as defined in articles 76 to 79 of the RAO;

Common accounts;

Certain funds relating to leasehold property;

Certain employee share schemes;

Schemes entered into for commercial purposes related to existing business;

Group schemes, i.e. schemes where participants are companies in the same group;

Franchise arrangements;

Trading schemes;

Timeshare schemes;

Other schemes relating to use or enjoyment of property;

Schemes involving the issue of certificates representing investments;

Clearing services;

Contracts of insurance;

Funeral plan contracts;

Individual pension accounts;

Occupational and personal pension schemes;

Bodies corporate etc. This exempts all companies other than open-ended investment companies, but the exclusion does not apply to any body incorporated as a limited liability partnership.

This list is set out in order to show the extent of the exclusions which are recognised. It is not desirable in principle and from a legal certainty perspective that regulatory definitions are vague and subject to many exclusions. Some of those exclusions, especially paragraphs 1, 2 and 5, are complex in themselves, and a scheme could fail to qualify for exclusion, and thus fall for consideration within the uncertain definitions of section 235.

Amendment or extension of the exclusions

Moving on from the consideration of the existing exclusions contained in the Schedule to the CIS Order, the next question is whether or not those exclusions should be amended or supplemented. Clearly, if the basic definition of a collective investment scheme is narrowed or more clearly defined, as considered in sections 3 to 6 above, then that will have a knock-on effect on the necessary scope of the exclusions. This section proceeds on the assumption that the basic definition is maintained.

Paragraph 9 of the Schedule

The principal focus of discussion to date has been on the redrafting of paragraph 9 of the Schedule. That paragraph excludes certain arrangements entered into for commercial purposes relating to an existing business. HM Treasury accepted that the scope of the current paragraph 9 is or could be perceived to be too narrow, and published two consultation papers, in January and August 2007, on the topic. Between these two papers a meeting took place at the Bank of England between representatives of the Treasury and of the FMLC Working Group, and we welcome and appreciate the extent to which our views expressed at that meeting were taken into account in the further consultation paper and in the amendments as finally adopted (the "Amended Provisions").12

It was common ground between the Group and the Treasury that the way forward was to redraft paragraph 9 rather than to exempt particular bodies carrying out property or commercial transactions. It was also common ground that amendment of paragraph 9 was preferable to the status quo. The Amended Provisions go a long way to meeting our concerns about the desirable scope and the drafting of an amended paragraph 9.

The first point made at the meeting and accepted in the second consultation paper is that the paragraph should define "permitted participants" falling outside the CIS regime rather than, as sub-paragraph (4) of the first draft of the amendment provided, saying that certain bodies are not participants at all.

Thus, in respect of new arrangements there is exclusion where all participants are permitted participants (as defined), absent agreement to the contrary in writing at the time the arrangement is entered into.

The second point reflected in the Amended Provisions is that the exclusion should not only be for participants who have a pre-existing business (other than or in addition to any business comprising specified regulated activities - "specified business"), but should extend at least to Special Purpose

Vehicles set up for the purpose of the transaction itself. In the event the Treasury has extended the range of permitted participants to cover all entities which do not carry on specified business and whose participants would themselves qualify as permitted participants if they participated directly in the scheme.

The third point which the Treasury has taken on board is the need to include non-legal persons. This is achieved in the following way. Of the two types of "permitted participant" the first, covering participants with existing businesses, makes no mention of extension beyond legal persons. The second, however, namely that considered in paragraph 7.8 above, expressly extends not only to corporate bodies, but also to an "unincorporated association, partnership or trustee (unless that trustee is an individual)". Limited liability partnerships are not mentioned, presumably because they qualify as "bodies corporate". The principal issue here is whether or not there is any need to extend the first type of "permitted participant" to include these non-legal persons.

The fourth point taken on board by the Treasury is the need to observe the requirements of Article 7 of the ECHR with regard to retrospectivity. Under the Amended Provisions that there be three categories.13 Existing CIS-exempt arrangements are to be preserved. Existing arrangements which do qualify as CIS should only be able to take advantage of the wider exclusion for the future where all participants irrevocably so agree and where they are "permitted

participants". New arrangements can take advantage of the wider exclusion, unless all participants agree irrevocably not to benefit from it. This seems to solve any retrospectivity problems.

The effect of these improvements to the amended paragraph 9 may be thought satisfactorily to address the concerns previously outlined. However, there is some room for argument about the words "wholly or mainly" which appear in the Amended Provisions. The idea is that a company which has a specified business should be able to benefit form the exclusion where it enters into an arrangement for commercial purposes "wholly or mainly" related to another existing business. There is some uncertainty here as to how this will operate, but it is probably acceptable, given the need to be able to protect those with specified businesses but also other businesses and yet to stay within the spirit of the proposed amendments.

It is worth noting that: In applying the paragraph in its present form the general view appears to be that "commercial purposes" is essentially a synonym for "business", or "money-making" purposes. In practice the FMLC understands that the exclusion is used in cases where at least some of the participants participate for what would naturally be characterised as investment purposes. It has to be assumed that the legislation does not intend to distinguish in this context between "commercial" and "investment" purposes as is the case, for example, in Articles 83 and 84 of the RAO (on options and futures, respectively). This view is convenient but not self-evidently correct; It will not always be easy to justify the participation of parties acting as trustee or nominee, since:It is at least arguable that trustees do not per se "carry on a business" at all, in which case they will not qualify as permitted participants except in the specific circumstances described in paragraph 7.8; A nominee may be engaged in the regulated activity of safeguarding and administering investments (article 40 of the RAO); and To qualify as in "indirect" participant a beneficiary of a trust will have to be involved in the overall arrangements for commercial purposes relating to the beneficiary's business

These points reflect a remaining uncertainty about whether the exclusion is meant only to cover "commercial transactions between businesses" (in the Treasury's words) or a wider range of joint transactions/investments involving financial and investment institutions.

Other exclusions

Other commonly-used exclusions either create their own uncertainty or exacerbate the practical difficulties of the general definition by being unduly narrow in scope. These are addressed below.

Individual investment management arrangements (paragraph 1)

This exclusion is designed to provide a partial answer to the problem of "parallel management" (see paragraph 3.14 above). An investment manager who manages a series of portfolios for individual clients in accordance with a standardised model will make acquisitions and disposals for each portfolio in accordance with the model and may thus be said to "manage [the property concerned] as a whole". The result may be that the overall arrangements constituting the manager's business in this area amount to a CIS, even though there is in substance no "collective" element.

To qualify for the exclusion the arrangements must (in summary) satisfy the following criteria:

The property concerned must comprise:

shares, debt instruments, warrants, or certificates representing securities, i.e. instruments falling within Articles 76 to 80 of the RAO; units in a regulated investment fund; a contract of long term insurance; or cash awaiting investment.

Each participant must be "entitled to a part of the property and to withdraw it at any time".14

There are various problems with these criteria:

305

there seems no reason why the range of permitted investments should be so limited. If this ever made sense, it does not do so in an investment environment where, for example, structured investment products (which are likely to fall within Articles 83 to 85 of the RAO) and unregulated hedge funds are widely used. If consumers need protection in dealing with those investments, this can be (and is) achieved in other parts of the regulatory system;

it is common for the assets managed under such a structure to be held by a custodian appointed by the manager. It is also common for assets in these circumstances to be held in a single account in the name of the manager, designated as held for the manager's clients. It is at least arguable that on the true legal analysis of such an account the clients concerned have an undivided share in the entire property. There is therefore some doubt about whether each of them is "entitled to a part of the property" it is not wholly clear whether an "entitlement to withdraw" must comprise a right to withdraw the assets in specie, or whether a right to realise their cash value is sufficient. To the extent that the client is not "entitled" to identifiable assets (see above) it is arguable that the reference to "withdrawal" of a part of the assets cannot be construed narrowly, but this is not clear.

Some liberalisation and clarification of the exclusion would remove uncertainty in this area.

Pure deposit-based schemes (paragraph 3)

This exclusion appears primarily designed to ensure that a bank or other deposit-taker is not a collective investment scheme. It applies where the whole of each participant's contribution is:

a deposit (presumably as defined in the RAO, though this is not stated) which is accepted by an authorised person with permission to accept deposits or an exempt person.

The oddity here is the restriction in (b). This implies that a non-UK bank may be a CIS. More generally there seems no good reason why a person who accepts deposits in circumstances which, presumably for good policy reasons, fall outside the scope of the regulated activity in article 5 of the RAO should then be made subject to the CIS regime.

"Schemes not operated by way of business" (paragraph 4)

The problem here is that there may be different views about what is intended by the phrase "by way of business". On a narrow view the exclusion will not apply if the operator is paid for its services. On a wider view the exclusion will apply if the scheme itself is not run as "a paying proposition". The distinction is important as arrangements where assets are commingled for purely administrative purposes, e.g. as a fund to make charitable payments, may be excluded on the wider view, but

not on the narrower view if a professional nominee
or administrator is used. 15

Further exclusions

We are not convinced that there is a pressing case
for the addition of any new categories, subject to one
exception. That relates to closed-ended collective
investment undertakings which are now covered by
the Prospectus Directive. Given that these
arrangements are fully provided for under that
Directive, there seems no need for them to be
regulated twice, i.e. under the FSMA CIS regime as
well. Not only is this duplicative, but also there is a
danger of inconsistency. Given that the opportunity
is being taken to review the scope of the exclusions,
it would seem that this is an ideal opportunity to
promote legal certainty by preventing an anomalous
and inconsistent result.

This leads to a broader point. The point taken in the
earlier paragraph about the Prospectus Directive
could be replicated in future as a result of further
changes in European law, where schemes of one
sort or another are brought within some form of
regulatory control, creating duplication with the
FSMA CIS regime. It would be useful to provide a
streamlined mechanism so as to enable such
anomalies to be dealt with without the need for the
introduction of a fresh statutory instrument.

BIBLIOGRAPHY

Michael Blair (ed), Blackstone's guide to the Financial Services & Markets Act 2000, 2001.

Deborah A. Sabalot, Richard J. C. Everett, The Financial Services and Markets Act 2000, 2004.

S. Gleeson, Retail Derivatives Made Simple, May 2003 International Financial Law Review, pp. 27-28.

FINANCIAL MARKETS LAW COMMITTEE MEMBERS

Lord Woolf, Chairman

Bill Tudor John, Lehman Brothers

Peter Beales, LIBA Sir William Blair Michael Brindle QC

Keith Clark, Morgan Stanley International Limited Simon Dodds, Deutsche Bank

Sir Terence Etherton, The Law Commission Ruth Fox, Slaughter and May

Ed Greene, Citigroup David Greenwald, Goldman Sachs

Mark Harding, Barclays Sally James, UBS Investment Bank

David Lawton, Financial Services Authority Clive Maxwell, HM Treasury

Gabriel Moss QC

Habib Motani, Clifford Chance LLP

Ed Murray, Allen & Overy LLP

Steve Smart, AIG Europe (UK) Ltd

Paul Tucker, Bank of England

Secretary: Joanna Perkins, Bank of England

SUELLA BRAVERMAN M.P.

HOUSE OF **COMMONS**
LONDON SWIA OAA

18 April 2018

Dear Janet,

Thank you for contacting me about the Solicitors Regulation Authority and EcoHouse.

As you will be aware, legal services in England and Wales are independently regulated in accordance with the framework set out in the Legal Services Act 2007. Solicitors are regulated by the Solicitors Regulation Authority (SRA), which prosecutes solicitors and firms involved in dubious investment schemes, as it has done in the Ecohouse case.

I should also highlight that the SRA and others have issued a series of warnings for the public and the profession to be wary of questionable investment schemes. While the legal profession is independent of government, it is the case that solicitors have a duty under their Code of Conduct to act in the best interests of each client, protect client money and assets, and not allow their independence to be compromised.

311

Similarly while HM Treasury sets the legislative framework for the regulation of financial services, the supervision and regulation of the financial services industry is a matter for the Financial Conduct Authority (FCA). The FCA is an independent, non-governmental body and HM Treasury cannot intervene in individual cases.

Investment in real estate is regulated by the FCA where it is undertaken as a consequence of having taken regulated financial advice, or by way of a regulated collective investment scheme. In 2014, the FCA prohibited the promotion of unregulated collective investment schemes, such as EcoHouse, and non-mainstream pooled investments to retail investors. On the same basis I should highlight that fraud is a criminal offence and as such is a matter for the police.

Thank you again for taking the time to contact me.

Suella Braverman

Member of Parliament for Fareham

Westminster Office: 020 7219 8191   Email: suella@suellabraverman.co.uk   Website: www.suellabraverman.co.uk

»@SuellaBraverman   I] Suella Braverman

Fareham Office: 14 East Street, Fareham, Hampshire, PO16 0BN. Tel: 01329 233573

SCHEDULE 5STATEMENTS FOR CERTIFIED HIGH NET WORTH INDIVIDUALS AND SELF-CERTIFIED SOPHISTICATED INVESTORS

PART ISTATEMENT FOR CERTIFIED HIGH NET WORTH INDIVIDUALS

1. The statement to be signed for the purposes of article 48(2) (definition of high net worth individual) must be in the following form and contain the following content—

I declare that I am a certified high net worth individual for the purposes of the Financial Services and Markets Act 2000 (Financial Promotion) Order 2005.

I understand that this means:

  (a) I can receive financial promotions that may not have been approved by a person authorised by the Financial Services Authority;

  (b) the content of such financial promotions may not conform to rules issued by the Financial Services Authority;

  (c) by signing this statement I may lose significant rights;

  (d) I may have no right to complain to either of the following

    (i) the Financial Services Authority; or

    (ii) the Financial Ombudsman Scheme;

  (e) I may have no right to seek compensation from the Financial Services Compensation Scheme.

I am a certified high net worth individual because **at least one of the following applies—**

  (a) I had, during the financial year immediately preceding the date below, an annual income to the value of £100,000 or more;

  (b) I held, throughout the financial year immediately preceding the date below, net assets to the value of £250,000 or more. Net assets for these purposes do not include—

    (i) the property which is my primary residence or any loan secured on that residence;

    (ii) any rights of mine under a qualifying contract of insurance within the meaning of the Financial Services and Markets Act 2000 (Regulated Activities) Order 2001; or

    (iii) any benefits (in the form of pensions or otherwise) which are payable on the termination of my service or on my death or retirement and to which I am (or my dependants are), or may be, entitled.

I accept that I can lose my property and other assets from making investment decisions based on financial promotions.

I am aware that it is open to me to seek advice from someone who specialises in advising on investments.

Signature   Date

313

PART IISTATEMENT FOR SELF-CERTIFIED SOPHISTICATED INVESTORS

2. The statement to be signed for the purposes of article 50A(1) (definition of self-certified sophisticated investor) must be in the following form and contain the following content—

I declare that I am a self-certified sophisticated investor for the purposes of the Financial Services and Markets Act (Financial Promotion) Order 2005.

I understand that this means

   (a) I can receive financial promotions that may not have been approved by a person authorised by the Financial Services Authority;

   (b) the content of such financial promotions may not conform to rules issued by the Financial Services Authority;

   (c) by signing this statement I may lose significant rights;

   (d) I may have no right to complain to either of the following —

      (i) the Financial Services Authority; or

      (ii) the Financial Ombudsman Scheme;

   (e) I may have no right to seek compensation from the Financial Services Compensation Scheme.

I am a self-certified sophisticated investor because **at least one of the following applies** —

   (a) I am a member of a network or syndicate of business angels and have been so for at least the last six months prior to the date below;

   (b) I have made more than one investment in an unlisted company in the two years prior to the date below;

   (c) I am working, or have worked in the two years prior to the date below, in a professional capacity in the private equity sector, or in the provision of finance for small and medium enterprises;

   (d) I am currently, or have been in the two years prior to the date below, a director of a company with an annual turnover of at least £1 million.

I accept that I can lose my property and other assets from making investment decisions based on financial promotions.

I am aware that it is open to me to seek advice from someone who specialises in advising on investments.

Signature   Date

Claim No: CL-2021-000051

Neutral Citation No [2021] EWHC 276 (Comm)

IN THE HIGH COURT OF JUSTICE

BUSINESS AND PROPERTY COURTS OF ENGLAND AND WALES COMMERCIAL COURT (QBD)

7 Rolls Buildings Fetter Lane London EC4A 1NL

Thursday 4 February 2021

BEFORE:

MR JUSTICE CALVER

BETWEEN:

CLAIMANTS LISTED IN SCHEDULE 1

- and –

(1) NICHOLAS SPENCE

(2) DEREK KEWLEY

(3) ANDREW CRUMP

(4) EMERGING PROPERTY INVESTMENTS
LIMITED (IN LIQUIDATION)

Defendant/Respondent

(5) EMERGING PROPERTY LIMITED

(6) GREEN PARK HOLDINGS (ILFRACOMBE)
LIMITED

(7) GREEN PARK (HOLDINGS) LIMITED (IN
ADMINISTRATION)

Defendants

Defendant/Respondent

(8) GP ILFRACOMBE MANAGEMENT COMPANY
LTD

(9) GREEN PARKS (WESTWARD HO!)
MANAGEMENT COMPANY LIMITED

(10) ALPHA PROPERTIES (BRADFORD) LIMITED

(11) A1 PROPERTIES (SUNDERLAND) LIMITED

Defendants

MR NEIL HEXT QC, MR MATTHIEU GREGOIRE and
MISS MELODY IHUOMA

(Instructed by Trowers & Hamlin LLP, 10 Colmore Row,
Birmingham, B3 2QD) appeared on behalf of the
Claimants

JUDGMENT

(As approved)

Daily Transcript by John Larking Verbatim Reporters

One Cow Lane, Church Farm, South Harting, West Sussex, GU31 5QG Tel: 01730 825 039

No of folios: 137 No of words: 9864

Thursday 4th February 2021

MR JUSTICE CALVER:

1. By this application the claimants, through Mr Hext QC, leading Matthiew Gregoire and Melody Ihuoma, invite the court to make a number of orders against the respondents on an ex parte basis without notice. Those orders consist, in particular, of a worldwide freezing order against the first, second and third defendants only (the injunction respondents) who, along with the fourth to eleventh defendants, the claimants wish to be the defendants to the underlying action, as well as supporting disclosure orders against the injunction respondents, and an order permitting the injunction as against the first defendant, if granted, to be enforced by way of parallel proceedings in Florida, United States of America.

2. The application is made without notice and on an ex parte basis, it is said to avoid the respondents being tipped off, which could trigger further dissipation of assets and undermine the relief sought.

3. Pursuant to CPR 39.23, I ordered this hearing to be held in private, as I am satisfied that publicity will defeat the object of the hearing and a private hearing is necessary in the interests of justice.

4. The background to this application is set out in the claimants' skeleton argument and is said to be as follows. The claimants are a group of individual investors – either individuals or corporate entities – who invested in holiday accommodation situated in Ilfracombe and Westbeach, Bideford, Devon, and in student accommodation in various locations in England, between 2012 and 2019. The claimants are represented by eight individual investors who are selected to form the Group Action Committee ("GAC") and who have overall responsibility for running the case on behalf of the claimants.

5. The first and second defendants are individuals who were the owners and/or controllers of several companies (together the Alpha Group) involved in the sale, management and letting of the properties at the material time. The Alpha Group includes the sixth to eleventh defendants, which were all incorporated in the United Kingdom. The first defendant presently resides in Florida, USA. The second defendant resides in England. The third defendant was at all material times the director and controlling shareholder, through his interest in XIP Capital Limited and XIP Holdings Limited, of the fourth

defendant, and a co-director and shareholder of the fifth defendant, the sole other co-director and shareholder being his wife. The fourth and fifth defendants were estate agents that marketed the properties exclusively at all material times. The fourth defendant has been in a voluntary insolvency process since 15th June 2020.

6. I am told that, given the number of claimants and the fact that instructions are provided by the GAC, where various assertions are made in the affidavit and skeleton argument that particular events followed a pattern, those assertions are derived from instructions from the GAC, evidence from individual claimants, reviews of samples of underlying documents across the relevant sites, and inferences that where no outliers have been identified from sample testing, the event or assertion applies to all claimants.

7. The claimants' investments were structured in the following manner. Firstly, a developer company (being members of the Alpha Group) would enter into an agreement for the sale of a leasehold interest in the property to the investor (the purchase agreement). The developer company would also enter into a long lease with, or assign a long lease to, each investor (the superior lease). Secondly and in turn, the superior lease was either concluded between a developer company, a designated management company and a claimant, or concluded between a freeholder, a developer company and a designated management company, and then assigned to a claimant. A long lease would then be granted over the property (usually 125 or 250 years), or where the developer company already held a long lease with the

freeholder, the leasehold interest would be assigned to the claimant. The investor would then be liable to pay rent and maintenance charges to the designated management company, and the investor was not to underlet the property, other than to a designated Alpha Group company.

8. Thirdly, at the same time as (or shortly after) entering into the superior lease, an investor would also enter into an underlease with a further Alpha Group company (the underlease holder). The underlease (a) provided that the investor let, with full title guarantee, the relevant property to the underlease holder for a fixed contractual term generally of ten years; (b) provided that the underlease holder was to pay to the investor amounts equivalent to the investor's liabilities to the developer company, and a fixed "Additional Rent" of between eight to twelve per cent, commensurate with the yield that had been represented to the investor; and (c) the underlease holder would then grant occupational tenancies to third parties when the properties were available for letting.

9. Each of the developer companies, the designated management companies and the underlease holders were all owned (or majority owned), whether directly or indirectly, and/or controlled by the first and second defendants, both at the time when the alleged representations were made to the claimants, to which I shall come, and at the time when the claimants made their investments. The sixth and eighth defendants were the developer and management company of the Ilfracombe site; the seventh and ninth defendants were the developer and management company for the Westbeach site; the

tenth defendant sold or assigned leaseholds to investors in relation to student accommodation; and the eleventh defendant was a seller or assignor of leaseholds to investors of student accommodation.

10. In the period 2012 to 2019, the properties were marketed by the fourth and/or fifth defendants, which were owned and controlled, I am satisfied, by the third defendant at the request of the first and second defendants. As a result, the claimants became aware of the investment schemes through various means between those dates, including through the fourth and fifth defendants advertising the properties on television, on the internet and by email. Further, the fourth and fifth defendants marketed the properties through brochures and other promotional materials such as prospectuses and investor reports which were communicated to the claimants prior to their purchase of the relevant properties.

11. The claimants' case is that the following express representations were made in respect of the student and holiday accommodation. There are five in number: first, representations that investors would receive a fixed return of between eight and twelve per cent for a fixed period of time (normally ten years); secondly, representations to the effect that the contracting counterparties were entities of substance, capable of paying the investors the fixed returns due; thirdly, representations to the effect that the developers had a strong and proven track record and an ability to pay the returns which were advertised; fourthly, representations to the effect that the returns were underwritten and therefore secure (that is, that there was an asset base against which one could enforce the sums

due – essentially, a form of security); and fifthly, representations to the effect that the properties which were already operational were fully occupied.

12. Mr Hext QC took me to the relevant brochures produced by the fourth and fifth defendants, where it is said that these representations were made. In light of the representations set out above, it is said that the brochures also contained various implied representations. These are set out in paragraph 22 of the claimants' skeleton argument. In addition to the representations in the brochures, it is also alleged that many individual claimants had telephone conversations and exchanged emails with the fourth and fifth defendants over the course of which the same representations were in substance reiterated.

13. The GAC is said to have established from the various claimants that on the basis of these representations they invested in the properties, and the investments were duly made between 2012 and 2019. Whilst some of the claimants initially received some payments commensurate with the yields that had been promised, between October 2018 and January 2019 payments ceased completely. At around the same time, the first and second defendants resigned as directors of the relevant underleaseholder companies.

14. Some of the claimants have been exposed to demands by the designated management companies for annual rent and maintenance charges which, according to the representations that it is alleged were made, should have been provided for by way of income from the underleases,

but which the claimants were now being required to fund from their own resources.

15. In late 2018, many of the claimants received correspondence from a Mr Sullivan on behalf of Alpha Group Entities or from the fourth defendant, suggesting that the developments were in financial difficulties. Eventually, the administrators were appointed in respect of the underlease- holder to the student accommodation, the parent company of the underleaseholder to Ilfracombe and Westbeach, and the underleaseholder of Ilfracombe. The underleaseholder of Westbeach went into voluntary liquidation on 8th July 2020.

16. The claimants alleged that the representations were false. In particular, they say:

(1) The Ilfracombe, Westbeach and student accommodation developments were never capable of generating the returns promised to the claimants;

(2) The underleaseholders do not have, and never have had, sufficient assets out of which to pay those returns;

(3) The returns are not, and were never, underwritten by any other entity, and there is no contractual recourse to any other entity or asset;

(4) Prior to the collapse of the investment schemes of which the properties form part, the returns paid to the claimants were funded, it appears, by the purchase consideration paid by other subsequent investors who

bought properties – in other words, it was a pyramid scheme;

(5) A number of the developments (or phases thereof) are in disrepair or are incomplete; and

(6) The properties are and were at all material times worth substantially less than the amounts the claimants paid for them. In a number of cases the properties, it is said, are worthless, and the total estimated value of the properties is £10.5 million, which is £44-odd million less than the total amount paid by the claimants.

17. The claimants' claim against the injunction respondents is for deceit and conspiracy to injure, as particularised in the draft Particulars of Claim. There is also a negligence claim.

18. I turn to the test for freezing orders. The court's jurisdiction to grant freezing orders derives from section 37 of the Senior Courts Act 1981. As Haddon-Cave LJ said in Lakatamia Shipping Company Limited v Toshiko Morimoto [2019] EWCA Civ 2203 at [33] to [34]:

"33. The basic legal principles for the grant of a WFO are well- known and uncontroversial and hardly need re-stating. It nevertheless is useful to remind oneself of the succinct summary of the test by Peter Gibson LJ in Thane Investments Ltd v Tomlinson (No 1) [2003] EWCA Civ 1272 at [21] where he stated that, before making a WFO, the court must be satisfied that:

'… the applicant for the order has a good, arguable case, that there is a real risk that judgment would go unsatisfied by reason of the disposal by the defendant of his assets, unless he is restrained by the court from disposing of them, and that it would be just and convenient in all the circumstances to grant the freezing order.'

19. It follows that, before making a worldwide freezing order ("WFO"), the court must be satisfied that:

(1) The applicant for the order has a good arguable case;

(2) There is a real risk, judged objectively, that a future judgment would not be met because of an unjustified dissipation of assets. There must be a plausible evidential basis for believing that any judgment would go unsatisfied by reason of the dissipation of assets; and

(3) It would be just and convenient in all the circumstances to grant the order.

20. I shall take each of these three conditions in turn.

(1) Good arguable case

21. The requirement for a good arguable case is not a particularly onerous one. The applicant need only establish a case which is more than barely capable of serious argument and yet not necessarily one which the judge believes to have a better than a 50 per cent chance of success: see Lakatamia Shipping.

22. The claimants will be bringing claims against the injunction respondents in the tort of deceit and unlawful means conspiracy. The ingredients for the bringing of an

action in deceit were summarised by the court in Schenk v Cook and Others [2017] EWHC 144 (B) at [83] as follows:

"… To found an action in deceit: (i) there must be a clear misrepresentation of present fact or law; (ii) the misrepresentation must be made knowingly, or without belief in its truth, or recklessly; (iii) the representation must be intended to be acted upon by the representee; and (iv) the representation must be relied on by the representee."

23. The claimants submit that the affidavit evidence produced by them on this application, which I have read, demonstrates a good arguable case against the defendants in deceit. It is necessary to take this submission in stages against each of the relevant defendants.

Alleged representations of fact

24. So far as the relevant representations are concerned, I consider that there is a good arguable case on the evidence before me for alleging the following:

(1) That each of the return representation, the substance representation, the underwritten representation, and the other express representation (that is the claimants' description of those representations in their skeleton argument) was made. In particular, as is apparent from the affidavits before me of the individual investors, as well as the affidavit of their solicitor, Mr Kenkre, that all claimants received an express representation to the effect that they would receive between eight and twelve per cent

net yields on the proposed investment made in the following form:

"Byers receive an effortless ten per cent net income fixed for ten years, with zero costs during this period."

There are a number of formulations of this wording, such as "an effortless and reliable income stream", "a fixed ten per cent income", but the gist is clear and is repeated in a number of the different brochures to which I have been taken.

(2) That the promotional materials contained in these representations, and marked "emerging properties" were provided to the claimants by the fourth and fifth defendants, and repeated in emails by their representatives. Accordingly, for the purposes of the cause of action in deceit, I am satisfied that the representations can be said to be made by the fourth and fifth defendants.

(3) That it is to be inferred that the information set out in the promotional materials, including the representations to which I have referred, was provided by or derived from information provided by the first and second defendants, who were the owners and/or controlled the development companies at the material times. Mr Hext has referred me to the Libyan Authority Investments v King [2020] EWHC 440 (Ch), where the court said at [104]:

"… where a representation had been made indirectly to a third party with the intention that it would be passed on to the claimant to be acted on by him, the representation was no less an actionable representation. …"

I agree.

(4) That in circumstances where the fourth and fifth defendants were acting as marketing agents for the development companies, an inference may be drawn to the effect that the first and second defendants intended that representations about the developments provided to the fourth and fifth defendants were to be passed on to potential investors. It is sufficient that the claimants are within the class of persons within their contemplation as likely to be deceived: see Standard Chartered Bank v Pakistan National Shipping Corporation [1998] 1 Lloyd's Rep 684 (at 696). Accordingly, the representations are to be treated as actionable representations made by the first and second defendants for the purposes of the claimants' claim in deceit.

(5) That the third defendant, as director and controlling shareholder of the fourth defendant, and a co-director with his wife, and a shareholder of the fifth defendant, will be held responsible for representations made by the fourth and fifth defendants if it can be shown that he directed, procured, or authorised the making of those representations.

The claimants have, in my judgment, a good arguable case that this requirement is satisfied. The third defendant was the sole director of the fourth defendant and co-director with his wife of the fifth defendant. It is likely, therefore, that brochures produced by the fourth and fifth defendants would have been issued with his authority. Indeed, his personal involvement is also suggested by his emails, to which I have been referred, that he sent to the investors. Moreover, it is apparent from an email, dated 2nd February 2016, from the second defendant to the third defendant that the second defendant himself gave the third defendant information about the development at the Box, Preston, including details of the underlease, and advised him to start to market the scheme.

Alleged falsity of the representations

25. Secondly, I turn to the falsity of the representations. I consider that that is a good arguable case that the representations were false. The claimants' investigations so far have revealed that that is likely to be so. As Mr Kenkre explains in his affidavit, the claimants instructed a company called CBRE to prepare a valuation report in respect of the properties which form part of the claimants' claim. As part of the process of valuing the properties, CBRE has reported on the likely levels of yield achievable by the properties. In short, they conclude – and the evidence does strongly suggest – that the investment schemes could never have produced yields of the levels represented in the promotional materials. There is also some powerful evidence to suggest that the first and second defendants must have known that to be so, not least the second defendant's own email to Quantuma, dated 24th June 2019, where he recognises the flaws in the business model. Furthermore, it appears that the properties are and were at all material times worth substantially less than the amounts than the amounts that the claimants paid for them.

26. CBRE's findings mirror those of Quantuma, who were appointed as administrators for, amongst others, A1 Alpha

Properties (Leicester) Limited, the underleaseholder in relation to the student accommodation, and Green Parks Holidays (Ilfracombe) Limited, the underleaseholder in respect of the Ilfracombe properties:

(1) By letter dated 29th May 2020, Quantuma concluded in respect of the Alpha properties that:

"What became apparent is that AlA had never generated sufficient profits in the past to meet the costs of ground rent and

service charge, and pay the additional rent. A1A had previously relied upon capital injections from associated development companies, presumably generated from the ongoing sale of further leasehold properties." (That is again a reference to the probability that this was a pyramid scheme.)

(2) By email dated 9th June 2020, Quantuma concluded in respect of the Ilfracombe site that:

"Financially the park never made a profit and returns to investors were not paid from genuine profits, but from funds paid in by Green Parks Holdings (Ilfracombe) Limited. As has been confirmed in writing, paying a fixed return is not a viable business model (never was), and as soon as sales of new units stopped, the entire scheme came crashing down."

Again, two points are made by Quantuma. The first is that this has all the hallmarks of a pyramid scheme; and the second is that the business model itself was flawed –

something which the second defendant himself recognised in the email of 24th June 2019, to which I have referred.

(3) Furthermore, it also appears that the contracts were not underwritten, as had been maintained in the promotional materials, and the underleaseholder was frequently not the developer and was never likely to be in the position to pay the supposedly fixed returns.

Defendant's knowledge

27. Thirdly, I turn to whether there is a good arguable case that each of the defendants is guilty of deceit. It is important to analyse the case against each of them separately. As against the first and second defendants, I accept that there is a good arguable case that the first and second defendants knew or must have known that the representations identified above were false; alternatively, that they had no honest belief in those representations, or at the very least were reckless as to whether those representations were true by reason of the fact that the first and second defendants were at all material times the owners (alternatively, the majority owners) and controllers of the Alpha Group, and were therefore the architects of the investments schemes, and were the sources of, or authorised the representations made by the third to fourth defendants. There is evidence, as I have said, that this was a pyramid scheme, and that they did not care whether or not the returns were capable of being made. On any view, there is a good arguable case, therefore, that they were reckless. They may say that they

can rely upon the disclaimer in the Sales Contracts, to which the Alpha companies were party; and that the investor has not relied upon any representation or statement by the seller. However, I accept the submission of Mr Hext in this regard, that such a disclaimer does not displace the serious allegation of deceit, which is advanced on the material in this case – certainly not so as to defeat a good arguable case argument.

28. They may also rely upon, as can be seen from correspondence between Quantuma and the first and second defendants, the Property Solutions Ltd 2015 Report on the Ilfracombe development, which suggests a return of eight to ten per cent to the investors, but there is significant doubt as to what materials the findings in that document are based upon. Indeed, neither the first nor the second defendant could justify the contents of that report when each was confronted about it by Quantuma.

29. Likewise, in relation to the Westbeach development, there is a Planning Solutions Consulting Limited document, also prepared by the same gentleman who prepared the Property Solutions Limited 2015 Report (a Mr Michael Stickland, about whom nothing is known), which raises the same sort of point about the return. However, that also suffers from the same failings as the Property Solutions Limited Report, in that it is difficult to understand, and certainly difficult to verify, the assumptions and the numbers which are contained within it.

30. Had the first and second defendants had a reasonable explanation as to how those assumptions and numbers were arrived at, no doubt they could have said when they were asked about it, but they did not. Accordingly, Mr Hext, for the claimants, says that it is not credible that the first and second defendants could have relied on these reports, or, if they did so, they were reckless to have done so. I accept that submission, certainly to the good arguable case standard.

31. So far as the third defendant is concerned, as director of the fourth defendant and co- director of the fifth defendant, it is said by the claimants that he knew the representations to be false; alternatively, that he had no honest belief in them; alternatively, that he was reckless as to whether they were true, such that the third, fourth and fifth defendants are liable in deceit.

32. What is the basis of this allegation? This is said to be so by reason of the fact that the third defendant was the sole director of the fourth defendant and co-director with his wife of the fifth defendant, which were the estate agents that marketed the properties exclusively at all material times.

33. It is then said that the fourth and/or fifth defendants' relationship with the developer companies was described in the brochure material as an "exclusive partnership". Indeed, in an email, dated 18th January 2016, to which I was referred by Mr Hext from Ross Thompson of Emerging Property to Janet Gafferana, an investor, the

fourth and fifth defendants describe themselves as "sole marketing agent" and they refer to what the partnership allowed them to do; indeed they refer to the fact that Alpha only became "involved in the PBSA industry with us from 2012". It is, therefore, presented that the fourth and fifth defendants are part of a partnership with the Alpha group to promote these schemes, and that this is not a normal vendor-estate agent relationship.

34. There is evidence, therefore, before me that the fourth defendant was involved in the scheme from the start, and that this was a collaborative venture with the first and second defendants.

35. The claimants also rely upon the fact that the Property Ombudsman found that there was no evidence to suggest that the fourth defendant had undertaken due diligence to ensure that all information presented in their marketing campaign was accurate and not misleading.

36. The response of Mr Crump (the third defendant) to this was to deny this. However, the difficulty with his response is that he accepted that he was provided with the terms of the contractual documents (the lease agreements) before he, the fourth and fifth defendants started to sell the units. If that is so, one asks the question: why did he not seek to correct his sales literature, because these documents fundamentally diverged in very important respects? Indeed, it can also be seen that his company was actually responsible for providing draft contracts to investors and arguably misleading them on this point: see the email of 1st June 2018, to which I was referred.

37. The documents put before me suggest that Mr Crump knew that the guaranteed rent was only as secure as the financial standing of the underlessee. That is apparent from Emerging Property's email of January 2016, to which I was referred, where it is stated that it is the developers' asset base which provides the security. But that appears to have been false. Mr Crump was at the very least, on a good arguable case basis, reckless as to whether or not this was true. Indeed, in one of Emerging Property's brochures there is a reference to competitors of Emerging Property signing contracts with SPVs, which is said to be not a secure method to adopt, precisely because those SPVs may subsequently have significant financial difficulties which render the investors' investments liable to be forfeited. In this case what was being said was that, in contrast, the investors had the security of the developers' strong financial standing to ensure that their investments were safe; whereas it is strongly arguable that Mr Crump would have known, having seen the relevant lease documentation which purported to give effect to the representations that had been made in the brochures, that that was not the case.

38. From all of this, I consider that to a good arguable case standard it can be inferred that the third defendant knew that the representations were false, or at the very least elected not to confirm that the representations were true and that he was therefore reckless as to their truthfulness.

39. The brochures of Emerging Property (the fourth and fifth defendants), to which I was taken by Mr Hext, contained, as I have mentioned, similar statements of fact,

such as the contracts having been signed directly with the established developer. I have already referred to the fact that it is strongly arguable that Mr Crump knew or ought to have known that that was not so when he received copies of the relevant underlying lease agreements. They also contained statements that there would be no third party shell companies, to which the same point applies. They also contained statements that ten per cent is to be paid by the developer (a company with assets). Again, the same point applies: it is strongly arguable that he knew, or ought to have known, that that was not true. The brochures also refer to these being "hand-picked properties" by the fourth and fifth defendants, "after thorough research underpinning our reports", and that buyers will "always receive their yields as expected, with the contracts aligned directly to the developer".

40. I agree with Mr Hext that there is at least a good arguable case to say that Mr Crump must have known those statements to be false when they were made; or at least he must have been reckless as to their truth. In many cases it is clear that the contracts were not underwritten by the developers' large asset base, as was represented in the brochures; rather, the contracts, if underwritten at all, were underwritten by SPVs, whose financial standing was not reliable, as indeed has transpired. There is a good arguable case that Mr Crump either knew that, or ought to have known that, in the light of the fact that he received the underlying lease documentation.

41. I accordingly consider that there is a good arguable case that each of the defendants is guilty of deceit.

Inducement

42. I turn next to inducement. It is plain from the nature of the misrepresentations and from the circumstances in which they were made, namely in the actual marketing promotional materials for the investment schemes, that they were made by the injunction respondents in a bid to induce the claimants to enter into the investment schemes. I accept, on a good arguable case standard, that the claimants have acted to their detriment in so doing.

Unlawful means conspiracy

43. The claimants also have a case in unlawful means conspiracy. I do not intend to say too much about that, other than because it is essentially based upon the same factual material, I consider that there is a good arguable case for an unlawful means conspiracy on the facts to which I have referred.

Quantum

44. So far as quantum of the claimants' loss is concerned, at present, on the basis of CBRE's analysis, the claimants maintain that they have sustained losses in the sum of almost £45 million in total, although there may be some reduction on that figure to take into account VAT. However, as Mr Hext says, the claimants also suggest that they have additional losses, which have not yet been particularised. That sum of around £45 million represents the difference between the value of the investment properties, assessed as at 9th September 2020, and the

sums paid by the claimants. The claimants also seek rescission of the purchase agreements and the superior leases.

Real risk of dissipation

45. I come next to the question of whether the claimants can prove a real risk of dissipation to the good arguable case standard. The claimants rely in particular upon paragraphs 346 to 374 of Mr Kenkre's affidavit, as well as the oral submissions made to me by Mr Hext today. The relevant principles were rehearsed by the Court of Appeal in Lakatamia, adopting the summary of the key principles applicable to the question of risk of dissipation by Popplewell J (as he was) in Fundo Soberano de Angola v Santos [2018] EWHC 2199 (Comm). Those principles, in short, are:

(i) The claimant must show a real risk, judged objectively, that a future judgment would not be met because of an unjustified dissipation of assets;

(ii) The risk of dissipation must be established by solid evidence, mere inference or generalised assertion is not sufficient;

(iii) The risk of dissipation must be established separately against each respondent;

(iv) It is not enough to establish a sufficient risk of dissipation merely to establish a good arguable case that the defendant has been guilty of dishonesty. It is necessary to scrutinise the evidence to see whether the dishonesty in question points to the conclusion that assets may be dissipated. It is also necessary to take account of whether there appear at the interlocutory stage to be properly arguable answers to the allegations of dishonesty.

(v) The respondents' former use of offshore structures is relevant, but does not itself equate to the risk of dissipation;

(vi) What must be threatened is unjustified dissipation. The purpose of a worldwide freezing order, I remind myself, is not to provide the claimant with security; it is to restrain a defendant from evading justice by disposing of or concealing assets otherwise than in the normal course of business in a way which will have the effect of making it judgment proof.

(vii) Each case is fact specific, and the relevant factors must be looked at cumulatively.

46. In assessing the risk of dissipation, is important to keep the defendants separate. The question is whether the risk of dissipation here is sufficiently solid. I consider that it is. As against each of the first, second and third defendants, I accept the claimants' general submission that the Defendants have been shown (to the requisite standard on this application) to have engaged in dishonest conduct, namely the perpetration of a fraud with the use of various company structures and that the fraud in question is such that it tends to show the defendants to be individuals who know how to use structures in a way which leaves victims with no recourse to funds. I emphasise, of course, that this

is the interlocutory stage, when I have not heard from the defendants.

47. In VTB Capital plc v Nutritek International Corp [2012] EWCA Civ 808, Lloyd LJ at

[177] said:

"We agree with Peter Gibson LJ that the court should be careful in its treatment of evidence of dishonesty. However, where … the dishonesty alleged is at the heart of the claim against the relevant defendant, the court may well find itself able to draw the inference that the making out, to the necessary standard, of that case against the defendant also establishes sufficiently the risk of dissipation of assets. …"

I so find here. In this case the alleged fraud was perpetrated through the use of a complex contractual structure which in the case of each investor involved at least three companies: the developer, the superior leaseholder, the designated management company and the underleaseholder, whereby the underleaseholder (the company with the obligation to pay investors returns on the investment and to discharge investors' liabilities under the leases) was a shell company holding no assets, contrary to the representations which had been made to the claimants.

48. In addition, Mr Kenkre points to the fact that the £55 million worth of funds invested by the claimants have been dissipated and that there are specific payments of those monies which merit particular concern, including service charge payments for the Alpha properties of

£830,000, in comparison to revenue of £1.3 million. Moreover, Mr Spence has paid in the region of $4.6 million in cash for three properties in Florida between March 2017 and January 2019 – the period of time with which we are most concerned; and Mr Kewley has also purchased a property in Florida. The timing of those transactions arguably corresponds with the relevant events with which we are concerned here, concerning the student and the holiday accommodation.

49. There is also some evidence to suggest that sums of money may have been moved by the first and second defendants to a new business operation in Florida, after the development schemes collapsed. Furthermore, once problems with each of the development schemes became apparent, the first and second defendants resigned their directorships of the relevant companies in or around late 2018, and for some time made themselves, it appears, uncontactable – certainly in December 2018.

50. So far as the third defendant is concerned, I originally had some qualms about whether the case was sufficiently proved to the relevant standard in so far as the risk of dissipation of assets on his part is concerned. However, having heard Mr Hext, I am persuaded that that risk to the relevant standard does also exist so far as the third defendant is concerned. In particular, he also used a relatively complex contractual structure to shelter his beneficial interests arising out of the scheme. He also has a serious case to answer regarding the dissipation of dividend payments to a company owned by him.

51. As I have mentioned, the fourth defendant's majority shareholder is a company known as

XIP Capital Limited. XIP Capital Limited and XIP Holdings Limited are jointly owned by Mr Crump; but the fourth defendant is the sole shareholder and director of XIP Holdings Limited – so, it all comes back to Mr Crump. The fourth defendant's Statement of Affairs shows that as at 1st June 2020 the only asset available for distribution to creditors was cash in the bank in the sum of some £22,000. That appeared to be offset by way of an unsecured loan owing to XIP Invest Limited, creating a net deficit of £27,000. The fourth defendant's accounts reveal that as at 31st August 2018, it had over £3 million in assets – debtors and cash at bank in hand – and over £2.5 million owed to creditors. So, as at 31st August 2018, the net current assets were some £515,000. As at 31st August 2019, it only had a net current asset position of

£26,000. It appears that significant funds had been paid out to XIP Capital Limited (Mr Crump's company) by way of dividends. So, in particular XIP Capital Limited's accounts for the year ending 31st March 2017, which showed a positive balance of £499,000, contained a note that dividends of £589,000 were paid from Emerging Property Investments Limited. At the year end, Emerging Property Investments Limited owed a balance of £300,000.

52. A year later, XIP Capital Limited's accounts for the year ended 31st March 2018 showed a positive balance of £1.191 million and a note that dividends of £780,000 were

paid out, and that at the end of the year Emerging Property Investments owed a balance of £991,500. Finally, in the following year, ending 31st March 2019, XIP Capital Limited's accounts showed a positive balance of just £3,000 odd. Section 5, entitled "Debtors", indicates that the amount of

£991,500 that was owed by the fourth defendant in 2018 was no longer owed by 2019. It is not known where those funds have gone, and the claimants allege that it is be inferred that the above fund movements were instigated by the third defendant, since he is the effective owner of XIP Capital Limited. Indeed, the timing of the removal of the money, when problems with these schemes were emerging, would appear to be significant. The fourth defendant then placed itself in voluntary liquidation, and the claimants invite the court to draw the inference that Mr Crump was aware of the potential for claims to be brought against him and the fourth defendant. So, he has taken steps to shield the fourth defendant from those claims: see paragraphs 369 to 370 of Mr Kenkre's witness statement.

53. It is true to say that there are factors which tend against any inference that the defendants are likely to dissipate their assets. In particular, so far as the third defendant (Mr Crump) is concerned, upon the collapse of the investment schemes early in 2019, and when the underleaseholders ceased to make payment under the underleases, he was contacted by a number of investors who wanted to know why payments had stopped. He wrote to the Ilfracombe investors via an email dated 4th January 2019, in which he said that he had been chasing

the first and second defendants since 22nd December 2018 to confirm that they would pay, but had had no response. He said that he had had a meeting with a Mr Sullivan, who I mentioned earlier and who was at that point the director of various Alpha Group companies. He then provided various updates to the investors. He will no doubt say that he sought to be helpful to the claimants, that he would disassociate himself from the actions of the first and second defendants, and he may say that this suggests that he did not know of any fraudulent scheme and was not a party to it. He would also no doubt say, as he said at the time in early 2019, that he lost money as well in the collapse of the scheme, and that he was not the cause of this.

54. The claimants, however, say that this was all too little too late; that what he was trying to do was position himself as the innocent party; and that it does not exonerate him from what went before, which is that he was involved in an arguable case of deceit and conspiracy.

55. Secondly, since July 2019 there has been press coverage, including in the Financial Times in relation to the matters which form the factual basis of the claimants' claim, and complaints have been raised by investors since early 2019. Indeed, there has been a settlement of some claims during this period, such that the defendants may well say that they have been aware for some time that a claim for fraud might be advanced against them, and so they are hardly likely now to seek to dissipate assets; that if they had proposed to do so, they would have it before.

56. In response to that argument, Mr Hext says: "We know they still have some assets, because they have been identified, and the issuing of proceedings against them is of a different magnitude to correspondence and press coverage and the like, and once proceedings are issued, bearing in mind the serious allegations of fraud which are central to the claim, makes it nonetheless likely that they will seek to dissipate their assets".

57. I accept the submission that the issuing of proceedings is of a different order of magnitude to the fact that there have been press reports of the investors' complaints and some discussions between the third defendant and the claimants. This fact, as well as the fact that there has been a settlement of some similar claims involving different claimants, is not sufficient to displace the other factors that I have referred to as supporting the solid inference that these defendants may well seek to dissipate their assets once proceedings are issued. Ultimately, the strongly arguable case in fraud which the claimants have established is at the heart of this claim and persuades me to draw the inference that these defendants are likely, once proceedings are issued and brought to their attention, to dissipate their assets or make it more difficult for the claimants to enforce any judgment entered against them.

58. Thirdly and finally, there is the issue of delay in the seeking of relief. Mr Kenkre has set out in his affidavit the steps that have been taken since Trowers and Hamlin were formally instructed in November 2019 by the GAC. Those steps led up to the claimant list being finalised on 11th September 2020. That list comprises 448 investors (treating joint owners as one investor), who collectively

345

own 672 properties across three types of development. Whilst there arguably has been some delay since the claimants' list was finalised on 11th September 2020, with this application not being launched until 27th January 2021, I accept the submission of Mr Hext that in circumstances where one is dealing with 448 investors, who collectively own 672 properties over three types of development, there is obviously a substantial burden upon his instructing solicitors to ensure that all of the relevant points that each of the investors wish to make are properly marshalled and placed before the court in a coherent series of affidavits, which is what has happened in this case. I accept that explanation.

59. In any event, delay per se is not a reason to refuse freezing injunction relief. As I shall mention, there remain sufficient assets which would make a freezing injunction worthwhile. In my judgment, the defendants are unlikely to be expecting to have their assets subjected to a freezing order. Since it is arguable to the requisite standard that they have shown themselves to be well capable of dishonest behaviour, once proceedings are issued, then as I have said I am willing, on the present evidence available to the court, to draw the inference that they are then likely to do whatever is necessary to shield their assets, including by seeking to render any judgment of the court valueless by an unjustified disposal of the same.

Existence of assets

60. I turn to the existence of assets. It is necessary for the claimants to establish that there are grounds for belief that the defendants hold assets on which the injunction will

bite, and I am satisfied that they do so. In particular, there are grounds for believing that the first defendant holds valuable assets, including four residential properties in Florida, USA, and by him jointly with his wife, Kerry Spence, with an estimated current value in the region of $5.2 million which, as I mentioned, he paid for in cash; four cars, including two Teslas, located in Florida; a Harley Davidson motorcycle, located in Florida; four boats in the USA, which were relevantly purchased between 2018 and 2020; an interest as a general partner of Alpha Developments (Orlando) LLP; and an officer of Colonial Apartments LLC in Florida. In particular, it appears that Alpha Developments (Orlando) purchased two lots at 3330 West Colonial Drive for almost $4 million cash in June 2019. Those lots were then transferred to Colonial Apartments in October 2019. That entity operates a motel business in Florida. It appears that he also has a 50 per cent shareholding in Barstow Projects Limited in the United Kingdom, and a 20 per cent shareholding in another company, F M Solutions Limited. In addition, of course, he has his interests in various Alpha Group companies.

61. The claimants also have grounds for believing that the second defendant holds valuable assets jointly with his wife, Kendra Kewley: in particular, 37 Ardsley Road, Stockton-on-Tees, which was purchased for £695,000 in November 2018; 33 Whitton Road, Stockton-on-Tees, which was purchased in 2006; a property in Florida, 14501 Grosvenor Resort Avenue, which was purchased in August 2017 for $324,000 in cash; and a Porsche car. He also has interests in various companies, separate from the

347

Alpha Group companies, in which he also holds interests. Indeed, it is interesting to note that, as with the first defendant, he appears to have an interest in Alpha Developments (Orlando) LLP and Colonial Apartments LLC, although the nature and value of his interest is unclear. It appears that that is a business in Florida in which he has an interest together with the first defendant, Mr Spence.

62. Finally, the third defendant and his wife purchased a property at Red Acre, Godalming in April 2016. That property is estimate to be worth around £1.5 million, although there appears to be a charge over it in favour of the Coventry Building Society. He may also be the owner of two BMW vehicles. The claimants believe that he may well also have assets in Romania, as is explained in Mr Kenkre's affidavit at paragraph 395. It also appears that he has paid out to companies which he owns, as I have mentioned, over £1.3 million in dividends declared by the fourth defendant. The timing of those payments is suspicious. It is not currently known where that money has gone. He also holds interests in various companies, although those interests do not appear to be particularly valuable.

Full and frank disclosure

63. I have taken account of the matters in paragraphs 76 to 101 of the claimants' skeleton argument, under the heading "Full and Frank Disclosure", and I have also heard Mr Hext's full submissions today, which have included, quite properly, a number of matters to which he has drawn my attention in terms of full and frank

disclosure being made to the court on this application. But I am satisfied that none of those matters should lead me to refuse to grant the freezing injunction which is sought.

64. I am satisfied that it is just and convenient that the relief be granted in this case. These are very serious allegations of dishonesty. I was told that the FT reported in June 2019 that more than 1,000 investors invested in these schemes a total sum of around £100 million. I am satisfied that these serious allegations meet the necessary evidential threshold for the granting of relief. If they are proven to be true, they have clearly caused very serious financial loss to numerous individuals. The fruits of this alleged dishonest course of conduct are easily dissipated, and I am satisfied that the balance of convenience weighs in favour of the order being granted, subject to the claimants' providing a cross-undertaking in damages, backed by an insurance policy provided by an A-rated insurer, GAC, which will provide an indemnity of up to £500,000 in the event of the undertaking being called upon, and which accordingly provides a safeguard against the risk of the injunction having been wrongly granted, as indeed will the draft order, which will allow the defendants to come back before the court to seek to have it discharged within a relatively tight timetable.

65. There remains also the points on which Mr Hext is to take instructions, as to whether or not the undertaking should extend to the wives of the defendants in view of the fact that they have interests, in particular, in some of the properties which are owned by the defendants.

66. I will hear Mr Hext on that, but those are my reasons for granting the freezing injunction relief.

(There followed a discussion on the order)

MR JUSTICE CALVER:

67. I shall briefly explain my thinking behind the service of the claim form and the ancillary documents and permission to enforce the injunction in Florida.

68. So far as service of the claim form is concerned, for all of the defendants domiciled in England, save for the first defendant who, as I have said, resides in Florida, the claimants intend to serve the claim form on those defendants who reside within the jurisdiction by leaving it at their usual or last known residence or, where they are corporate entities, at their principal office or any place of business of the company within the jurisdiction which has a real connection with the claim, in accordance with CPR Rule 6.9.

69. Although he is resident outside the jurisdiction, the first defendant is a director of a number of English companies and so the claimants are entitled to serve the claim form on him at the address under which he is registered at Companies House, under section 1140 of the Companies Act 2006: see Idemia France SAS v Decatur Europe Ltd & Ors [2019] EWHC 946 (Comm). Since the first defendant can be served with the claim form and particulars of claim within the jurisdiction, permission is not required to serve these injunction-related documents

on the first defendant personally out of the jurisdiction: see CPR 6.2(c) and the note at paragraph 6.2(3) of the CPR. The reference to "claim" includes an application before action. A pre-action application is treated like a claim form.

70. In case that is wrong, then the court grants permission to serve all the documents associated with the worldwide freezing injunction, including any freezing order that is granted, on the first defendant personally out of the jurisdiction in Florida.

71. In order to obtain permission, the claimants are required to establish that there is a serious issue to be tried on the merits of the claimants' claim against the first defendant; that there is a good arguable case that one of the gateways set out in Practice Direction 6B applies; and that England is clearly and distinctly the appropriate forum to try the case. I have already found that there is a serious issue to be tried on the merits of the claim for the same reasons that there is a good arguable case on the merits. The claimants are then entitled to rely on two of the gateways set out in the Practice Direction 6B. First of all, Practice Direction 6B, 3.1(3) which states:

"(3) Where a claim is made against a person (...) on whom a claim form ... will be served and –

(a) there is between the claimant and the defendant a real issue which it is reasonable for the court to try; and

(b) the claimant wishes to serve the claim form on another person who is a necessary or proper party to that claim."

72. The second gateway is the tort gateway, Practice Direction 6B, paragraph 3.1(9): "(9)A claim is made in tort where –

(a) damage was sustained, or will be sustained, within the jurisdiction; or

(b) damage which has been ... sustained results from an act committed ... within the jurisdiction.

73. I consider that both of these gateways are satisfied. So far as the first gateway is concerned, the second defendant is domiciled in England and there is a real issue between the claimants and the second defendant which it is reasonable for the court to try. The first and the second defendants are said to have been parties to a dishonest, fraudulent scheme, and so that gateway, it seems to me, is satisfied.

74. Secondly, the tort gateway is also satisfied. The loss sustained upon entry into a transaction as a result of a misrepresentation is the loss upon the making of the financial instrument, and the claimants have sustained economic loss here in paying monies to the fourth and fifth defendants, and indeed to companies operated by or on behalf of the first and second defendants. In any event, damage has also been sustained as a result of misrepresentations made within the jurisdiction. In a case that is based on misrepresentation the relevant act is committed where the misrepresentation is made. So the

damage here is the results of acts committed within the jurisdiction.

75. Similarly with the unlawful conspiracy claim, it seems to me that there is a good arguable case that the conspiracy was hatched within the jurisdiction, within England. Two of the parties to the conspiracy were domiciled in England at the relevant time and it is likely that any communications between them would have taken place in England. That is clearly the appropriate forum for the trial of the dispute. English law is the applicable law of the claim and Article 4 of Rome II provides that the law applicable in respect of a tort shall be the law of the country in which the damage occurred which, as I say, is England. Indeed, the facts relevant to the causes of action in deceit and conspiracy to injure all took place in England. Most of the witnesses will clearly be based in England as well, although that is a lesser consideration these days with the use of technology. It is likely that identical (or substantially identical) facts will be alleged against the first defendant to those that are alleged against the second defendant. Since the second defendant is domiciled in England and will be served here, the court will have jurisdiction in respect of the claim against the second defendant, and it is obviously sensible that the first defendant should be tried in the same action to avoid the risk of inconsistent judgments. I do not think I need to grant permission to serve out, but if I do, I grant it.

76. So far as permission to enforce the injunction by parallel proceedings in Florida is concerned, I grant that

application. The principles which govern the application are set out in the Court of Appeal's judgment in Dadourian Groups International v Simms [2006] EWCA Civ 399 [25]. The claimants have obtained advice from an attorney practising in Florida, Mr Rodz, who is a partner at Shoots & Bowen LLP. His advice is that the courts of Florida routinely enforce injunctions entered by foreign jurisdictions, applying principles of comity, and it is understood that a foreign order is entitled to comity where the parties have been given notice and the opportunity to be heard; secondly, where the foreign court had original jurisdiction; and, thirdly, where the foreign decree does not offend the public policy of the State of Florida. Two and three are satisfied here, I am told. As far as the first of those requirements is concerned, that is also satisfied because Florida law allows for the issuing of ex parte injunctive relief, provided that the respondents to such an order will later receive notice and have an opportunity to challenge the order before the foreign court, as they can here.

77. I accept that it is just and convenient to grant permission to enforce the worldwide freezing order against the first defendant, and indeed the second defendant in Florida, in circumstances where a substantial proportion of the first defendant's assets are held in Florida and indeed he resides there. Similarly, the second defendant, as I have mentioned in my earlier judgment, has assets in Florida. The urgency which justifies the making of the freezing injunction application also provides the basis for the claimants' application without

notice to the first defendant and the second defendant for permission to enforce the freezing injunction in Florida.

78. Accordingly, I grant this application and, as I understand it, the intention of the claimants is to obtain the ex parte order in Florida and, having obtained that, then to serve all of these proceedings upon the defendants in England and in Florida

79. Finally, so far as permission to bring a claim against the fourth defendant is concerned, I do not grant that application. It seems to me that it would not be appropriate to make such an order on a conditional basis and without knowing the precise circumstances which currently obtain in the liquidation and indeed hearing, if necessary, from the liquidators. In any event, the claimants can serve their proceedings against the fourth defendant because I am told that they have no reason currently to believe that there is any impediment in that respect.

80. So far as the permission to bring a claim against the seventh defendant is concerned, I am not minded to grant that app

Printed in Great Britain
by Amazon